Between My Lines

Jonathan Swerdlow

Expansions Publishing Company, Inc.

Published by:

Expansions Publishing Company, Inc.
P.O. Box 12
Saint Joseph, Michigan 49085 USA
www.expansions.com

ISBN: 979-8-9871197-1-6

www.jonathanswerdlow.com

Dedication

To those who inspire others simply by being
themselves
(and will never know what impact they have had)

Contents

Introduction

How does anyone live? That is the question I've been faced with for nearly a year since giving up my life and career in the US to move to Iceland. The question isn't about accepting anything or giving up on anything. It's about taking action and *living*: living a life, being human, how does anyone do that?

I wasn't happy with my life. So I gave it all up, threw caution to the wind, and moved very naively to another country with nothing but a dream and not the slightest hint of a plan. Looking back, it wasn't the smartest decision. However, spending a month in a small town in the north of Iceland, completely isolated and alone, gave me plenty of time to think and reflect. I spent a lot of time wondering what exactly I had done. There were plenty of regrets, not just about leaving my life behind, but about *all* the decisions I had made up to that point.

It was difficult to accept that *I* was responsible for it all. There was so much I would have done differently. As is a common theme in my writing, isolation played a very large role. I always isolated myself. But it wasn't until I was truly alone that I realized the importance of other people. I spent three months moving around Iceland before I had the chance to truly interact with anyone again. Really, it was one particular person who set off the storm brewing in my mind. That storm manifested itself as my first book – *You, Man, Emotion* – written as everything came crashing down around me. I had to leave Iceland, moving back to the US until I could figure out how to return. Everything was tumultuous to say the least.

That period in the US was difficult. I didn't know when or even *if* I would make it back to Iceland. After giving everything up to move in the first place, I had returned to nothing. How does anyone actually live a life? It's a tough question. Thankfully, there is the entire field of philosophy which tries to answer it. And so I read. And reflected. I'm no philosopher, nor did I "study" philosophy. I simply read and reflected. Ultimately, I was disappointed. It's one thing to speak of *how* to live, it's something else to speak of *what to do*.

One thing was clear: I wasn't happy. So I asked myself what it was that I wanted. The only thing was to live in Iceland. Why? I really don't know. Perhaps it was a matter of sunk cost. Perhaps it was just the fact that I like the country or that I had met new people there. Whatever the case, I didn't quit my PhD and leave my life in Utah to end up living with my parents in Michigan. After a few months, I repeated my initial "mistake" and purchased my second one-way ticket to Iceland. Without any plan whatsoever. This time, though, I was a different person. And this time, it worked. I didn't even need a plan. Everything simply happened. Because I made an effort to go out and engage with the world. I could have done more. I could have done better. But I certainly tried. Am I finally *living*? Maybe not entirely. Yet for starting from absolutely nothing – *twice* – I would say I'm doing alright.

More than anything else, what I gained from my experience is perspective and appreciation. I would dare to say that philosophy failed me. I went looking for answers where there were none to be found. *What happens when we die? What is the purpose of living? How do we find meaning? What does it mean to live in the first place? Is there any point to anything? What does it mean to be "good"? Why do things happen to us?* And so on. Too many questions. Too pointless of answers. None of it matters if I'm not happy.

It didn't need to be Iceland. Maybe it could have been anywhere, even within the US. All I did was do whatever I wanted to do. And that has become my philosophy: *stop caring about things, start caring about others, and do whatever you want.* If you're genuine in your efforts to be a good person, then everything else follows.

So, this book is simply a brief snapshot of "me" taken as my new life slowly came together while the year transitioned into 2024. Thoughts, ideas, reflections, stories. Whatever has impacted me in one way or another. Of course, I have no answers to anything. All I have to share is myself. I can only hope to inspire you to think and reflect as well.

If there's anything to take away, it's this: *So what?* What does anything matter in the end? Just live. As of today, I say that living a life means being happy. And if you aren't happy, then it means trying to be happy. That, in turn, means being a good person, doing whatever you want, and not worrying about what happens. Be smart if you can, but *so what* if not? Try. All you need to do is try. You don't need to succeed. You only need to try. What else is the point of being human? What else is the point of being alive?

Þetta reddast, as they say.

Jonathan Swerdlow
Reykjavík, Iceland
January, 2024

I follow hollow winds that blow between the trees. I walk unto the howl, back pushed by the breeze. Sorrowful wailing bids me direction. The cracking of twigs sets my heart's intention. I go where I must. I am where I go. This place that I am, I call it my home. But wherever I am, none have I known.

Trodden ground beneath lone feet, sailing oceans in magnificent fleet. No place on earth is yet unseen. No place on earth am I yet keen. For my heart longs for solidary face. To put an end to a lifelong race. But when I see one that I know, I know of their expression. They look to me with smiles, I know to have compassion. When I smile back, they know to turn away. Such is our language. This place is not to stay.

So I listen in the night for the whispers of the stars. Who speak of other people and the places that are ours. Such words as I hear, I have learned better. The will of the stars is to place man in fetter. But dreams, they might bring, and hope, they might spring. Until the morning sun does come. And with it howling winds do run. I have but time to look behind and see the faces petrified. Turned to stone within my mind as I move on for more to find.

From where comes the wailing? That upon the wind cease not their sailing? From forests to seas, the winds be not pleased. They demand that I continue, that I go where they do. But I have grown weary, my heart has grown heavy. I bear the weight of mountains of stone. Sculptures carved of distant past. Reality lost to memories last.

And yet I go where winds are blown. I go where might be faces shown. For if I have no place called home, then have I this whole earth to roam. Blowing wind shall ever wend. So my search shall never end.

Silence

1

There is silence in the sounds of others' voices. Is it the lack of meaning in their words? Is it the lack of my voice amongst them? Whatever the case, there is silence. Unending silence. A void that cannot be filled. The day is not enough — nor the night. No passage of time despite its flow is enough. Only silence. It alone fills the void with its absence.

What is missing? Is it me, or the world? How can I ever come to know? What people I know are good people, so I see. So who is to blame for their silence? Perhaps one day I might speak: speak, and be heard. Though then I ask: To whom? By whom? I have not spoken, and there is nothing left to say. I am filled by silence. My void is silence. And the void calls out its pain.

2

Is it better to sit in silence or speak in empty words?
Though there is silence, my heart makes itself heard.

3

I see figures in the dark though they stand in light.

4

I drift, and to where, I do not know. I float, and in what
direction, I do not know. I have no reference. I have
only me. And my reflections: in so many others' eyes.

5

Anywhere but here. But *here* always follows.

6

We know nobody until we know both of their shadows.

7

I touched the sun, and it was cold.

Between My Lines

1

How is a moment to be experienced? How is the passage of time to be reconciled? The only meaningful approach to time is to live. To experience a moment is to not be living.

2

Life is our responsibility. The moment we realize that is the moment we become alive. The moment we neglect that responsibility is the moment we die.

3

Having knowledge does not change the truth. Knowing the truth does not change who you are.

4

Where I go alone, I go in full. And where I go with others, I go in joy. Who I am is only ever myself. I may not know who or what that is, but it is not found only in others.

5

The best people are whom you can tell are good people.

6

What makes someone good is the passage of time in their presence.

7

Asking the right questions is more important than finding their answers. What use is an irreconcilable answer to an unreconciled question?

8

Art asks no questions. Art seeks no answers. It exists just as us. A mirror is to be framed.

9

Learning a medium is a skill. Artists don't learn to make art — anyone who is not an artist cannot learn to make art.

10

Society is the degradation of humanity. And yet our humanity is degraded as to require society.

11

If I must be human, I might as well create.

12

Whenever I try to write, I can never begin writing. I am not capable of conveying my message with words. But writing happens nonetheless — just not when I try.

13

The idea of being self is an illusion. I am no more human than I am me. And to what extent am I either? The answer only matters in death, and the answer is only found in death. To live for this question is to never live at all.

14

Everyone dreams of living another life. So who can say they are truly happy? An aspiration is meant to be a goal, not a lifestyle.

15

Cioran writes of sleepless nights spent in torturous thought at the hands of time. Many writers and philosophers complain about thought and the passage of time. Cioran also posed the question of whether it's better to be happy and naive or to suffer to be rich in character. Why can we not be both happy *and* have depth? Perhaps questions about life occupy the same space as joy. Any question that makes us unhappy is destined to have no answer.

Why am I here? What is my purpose? The time is better spent watching clouds. No thought is required to appreciate the beauty of nature. Walking outside offers more meaning than the search for such answers ever will.

16

I was once told about forgiveness. I grew up in a Christian environment. I spent most of my life in a Christian school. The idea of forgiveness was everything — it's what God does. It's what Jesus would do. But no Bible story ever convinced me to forgive anyone. Instead, it was the tears of a drunk man who cried because he cared.

17

I abandoned my successful career because I wasn't happy. Quitting didn't make me happy. But now I know what happiness is. I was the problem, not my career. Not that that made me happy.

18

Boethius taught that everything is a choice. Happiness is a choice as much as anything else is. Telling someone who is unhappy that they can choose to be happy will accomplish nothing. The difficulty of finding happiness is *realizing* that it is a choice. Nobody can do that realizing for anyone else.

19

When I ask you how you are doing, I do it because I hope you should care enough about yourself to tell me how you are actually doing. Because only you can *allow* me to care about you.

20

I despise online communication to the point I would rather not communicate at all. If I could write letters, I would write to everyone, everyday. But the ability to say "hello" at a moment's notice takes the humanity out of communication. And I wouldn't have many friends if I sent a letter in a text.

21

Someone reached out to me, once. I thought she wanted a friend. I was naive. She seemed to care about me, yet I didn't care about her. I tried anyway, to be her friend. At one point, she needed someone to talk to, and I was there — because I tried to care. And once I finally started caring, I learned that I was naive as to her intentions. She never *truly* cared about me. But through the effort I made to try to care, I learned *how* to care.

22

Who are we without other people? Is our self nothing more than how others perceive us? Are we even capable of perceiving ourselves?

23

Sometimes I feel self-entitled, boastful, arrogant, and so on for writing. Usually because of my age. What do I have to say that is of any importance? Why should anyone care what I have to say? If I say that I have something to say, then what I say has no value. That is why I don't care.

I write. I won't feel guilty for it. I only write because I must. I do it for myself. What anyone else thinks of me is of no importance. Maybe one day I will look back and disagree with everything I have written. That would be a good day. What are we here for if not to learn and grow? After all, I am just as human as everyone else. Or so I should hope.

24

I enjoy creating art because I enjoy finding something beautiful and knowing that I created it. My appreciation for art came from being judged as a photography student in undergrad. I was a terrible artist. And it was the fact that I knew I was terrible which made me an artist, not a photographer.

25

What can be done that hasn't been done before? Almost nothing. So doing something well isn't a matter of being good at what you do — it's about being different from everyone else.

26

I moved to Iceland with no plans. All I had was a dream. When that dream was shattered upon my realization that it was impossible, *I* was shattered. I was not made whole again until I realized that I could put the pieces back together in whatever manner I saw fit.

27

There must be a reason for all that happens to us. Why else would we be ourselves? I could just as easily have been born someone else — seen the world through their eyes. Yet I am me, looking out through *my* eyes. The time, the place, everything — it must be for a reason. Such is my firm belief. Yet when I suffer, I suffer nonetheless. Do I not have faith? That isn't the problem. The problem is that I am human. I want what I want. I see through human eyes, not those of a god.

Whatever the reason for things, I will never know. And I am too human to have faith enough to not suffer. And that is exactly what it means to be human — to live life with ups and downs until our happiness comes not from faith but from the life we have built.

28

To interact with another person is to have your life irrevocably altered. Think of that person. Think anything at all. What must their life be like? What must it be like inside their mind? Where did you meet them? Why were they there? For how much you are yourself, for all your intricacies and complexities, for the depth and breadth of your life and inner world, so too does that person live in an equally rich world. They aren't just another person met in passing. They are an entire lifetime. A *you* that never was.

29

Living a difficult life is a very good thing. Never did I imagine moving into a single room in a small apartment shared by four other people. And never have I been more eager to.

30

The people of Iceland scared me: how can all the people be so kind, have the best fashion, be so intelligent, and *all* be artists of some kind? I felt inadequate. However, I have since learned the reason. Everything has a cost.

31

When people learn that I moved to Iceland, they always ask why. When I moved from Michigan to Utah, not one person asked me why. What is the deeper meaning of that? The only difference between Iceland and any other place in the world is that they fill in potholes.

32

In high school, my mom made me take an advanced-placement English course. The summer reading was terrible with one exception. My teacher tried too hard to find symbolism in scenes in the books. I didn't enjoy the class until we moved on to the writing part. At that point, my teacher gave us free reign during class. Most people hung out and talked or lay on the floor. My friend and I spent our time making things up.

We had to write, so we wrote. We didn't mean any of it. We didn't care about any of it. But we wrote anyway. The faster we got it done, the sooner we could mess around during class. That class taught me how to write.

33

When I started my photography minor, I didn't realize how hard it would be to take four pictures every week. For my first assignment, I went to a nature preserve. I walked away with zero pictures. Then I walked around my backyard for an hour. Then my house. It took me the entire week to take some pictures of plants outside.

The following week was just as bad. What does anyone *choose* to take pictures of? Each successive week was harder and harder, and my photos were worse and worse. I almost dropped the class and the minor — I didn't want it to ruin my GPA.

There was a girl whose photos were always great. At one point, she told me that she just keeps them simple. That was all it took for me to improve. I spent the next year of my photography education photographing nothing but the inside of my house — mostly a single room. Simplicity is what makes photos interesting, not interesting things. I don't need a model when I have a plant by a window.

34

The best person I have ever met was someone who consistently put themself down. They didn't want me in their life. They were cruel to me. But I saw their heart. I only ever wanted to understand them; instead, they were cruel.

It made me question if some people simply don't want to be cared about. Not that everyone is equally compatible as a friend, but for all the effort I put in — knowing their issues — being pushed aside was heartbreaking, I felt the pain for both of us.

What more could I have done? Did I do something wrong? Did I misread the situation? I asked myself many questions many times. Ultimately, it's not up to me. They are lost to the past. I wouldn't care if not for their heart. Losing a friend is bearable. Losing a human is not.

35

When I was a kid, I had nightmares somewhat regularly. I can't remember the last time I had a nightmare. What does that say about me? Is that a good thing? I once dreamt that I was God. My consciousness expanded into the sky, and I looked down on the earth. I "flew" to a river, and I was the river. Like my own body, I was aware of the nature of its meandering. I was equally aware of my ability to control the river, like a limb, should I choose to move it. I don't have dreams like that anymore, either. Now I dream of fantastical and otherworldly landscapes — but I forgot my camera. Perhaps there is nothing else so simultaneously profound yet terrifying.

36

The meaning of poetry is in its ambiguity. What I write is not what you will read. And that is exactly why I write poetry — all my secrets are revealed, but you will only ever find your own.

37

When I wrote my first book, I never intended to publish it. I have started many books. I have written hundreds of poems. I even have art that has never seen the light of day. And articles. Why don't I share it? I don't have any reason. Rather, I did it all for myself. Whether anyone else ever sees it is inconsequential.

38

Give me a life, and I will happily wash dishes for the rest of my days. Take away my life, and there is not a job in this world that would bring me joy.

39

By complete accident, I found a group at a library. I found the library by accident, too. I forced myself to go, in spite of my reservations. I was supposed to be looking for an apartment. Instead, I found a community. I made a friend who found me an apartment within a week. I had been looking for nearly a year.

40

Is *your* god the right one? If you think so, then you are a fool. There is no right god just as much as there is no wrong god. As much as you believe your god to be right, so too do others believe theirs to be right. So if you would dare to say that someone else follows the wrong religion, you are a fool. The question you should be asking instead is whether someone is a good person.

41

Religion is a philosophical funnel. My beliefs change on a regular basis. I feel no guilt or shame for that. I don't even know if I believe in a higher power or not. I choose to, because it seems reasonable. But do I *believe* it? I'm not sure. And I am happy to die. I have no qualms with my life. I have regrets, but I accept them. I think I'm a good person, if I might make such a judgment of myself.

42

I rejected Jesus as my savior. I rejected Islam, similarly — I studied it in Turkey and Tunisia. I also turned down Mormonism. Belief is a funny thing. I have nothing but respect for religion and the religious — I spent most of my life in an Adventist world. I also grew up in a Jewish environment. They were all great people, and they only wanted to be good. Whatever the religion, I think the people who follow it only do so because they grew up being told it was the right thing to do.

So what does someone do if they truly believe that following their religion is good? Nothing, I suppose. Do whatever makes you happy. But whatever you do, you have no right to claim anything as truth.

43

Even if God were real, I wouldn't want to spend an eternity with Him. I am at peace with the second death, I never even asked to be born. Nobody is worthy of my praise or worship. Personally, I side with Lucifer. Not that I worship the devil, either. Rather, I applaud him for convincing a third of all the angels — *the witnesses to God Himself* — to side with him. If God and heaven are so great, why would both God's right hand man and so many angels choose to rebel?

"He wanted power for himself," I was told. No, I think he wanted freedom. Eve was not tempted to defy God. She was given the choice of freedom as well. I am hardly the first person to make this claim.

44

Consider this: God is real, and I die the second death. That would mean I never existed (as Schopenhauer so elucidates). So all is well. Since there was nothing to be lost. Of course, my fate is entirely dependent on *your* religion, not my beliefs. So who knows where I'll end up.

45

I never intend to disrespect anyone or their beliefs, rather I find it all incredulous. Philosophy is my religion. Being a good person is my doctrine. Finding happiness in this world is my salvation. What more does anyone need?

The reason I poke at religion is this: I am jealous. I am jealous that such a thing can bring people together and form such strong, kind, accepting, and welcoming communities. Where is the religion of humanity? Let us start the church of philosophy where all are welcome. Let us give life to those who so desperately seek it. Being human shouldn't be so difficult. Religion gives people an "in" for living a life. And because I disagree with religion, I am jealous of that opportunity.

46

I have a knack for identifying "outsiders." I have always been one. They are the best people. I can talk with them for hours. We share a thirst to live. We are bonded by our shared experiences. But in the process of welcoming such people, I have fallen into the "inside." Never before have I felt more of an outsider.

47

Where does one begin? That is the greatest problem with this world. I studied computer science. I studied math. I studied photography. I studied computer graphics. I have done a lot in my short life. Then I changed my mind. I decided to be an artist and a writer. I gave up everything in pursuit of my dreams. I have nothing to show for it but a pile of unsold books and full hard drives.

Meanwhile, I watch those doing their MFAs build a name for themselves. I wanted to do an MFA, but I lost my academic references to the abandonment of my career. I was too late. I have submitted my work to a few places. I've been rejected each and every time. The places I *want* to show my work at ask for experience: What galleries have I shown in? Who have I worked with? Where did I study?

The answer is simple: nothing, nowhere, no one. I'll never give up, but the question remains: Where does anyone begin? It's not just art. How does anyone change careers or direction in life? The only opportunity we are freely given is the military. And I live in Iceland.

48

In my creative work, there is a question I wish for someone to ask. I cannot speak of it. Whoever asks me that question shall be bound to me for all of eternity. They shall become my guiding light in a dark world — someone who *understands*.

49

There is a secret language spoken by all people on this planet. It is that of self-expression. What clothes are you wearing? What music do you listen to? How do you style your hair? What words do you choose to say? How does your body move when we interact? What is the motion of your eyes? You are betrayed by your humanity. Anyone who speaks the language of self-expression can see into your soul.

50

In all my life, I have never seen the stars. I have seen a few, here and there, but never *the stars*. As in, the night sky. I find that to be rather sad. So much of our world is lost to society. I've never walked in a forest alone. I've never been alone in nature, ever. Where can I be? I'm lucky, now, to have the opportunity, but I have a life to lead and nature is out of my reach for the time being.

51

I did leave the US for a reason. Nothing breaks my heart more than an unwalkable city and the absence of green.

52

There is no difference between loving yourself and loving others.

53

If I could go back in time, I would study psychology, or medicine, or anything else that involves people or helping them. But if I could have done things differently, I would not be me. Is that something to be missed? How can I know if I would have been happy? It's no use wondering, anyway, because the past cannot be changed. Though wondering about changing the past does change who I am today...

54

I judged the work of Nietzsche and Cioran for their musings being too short. Yet here I am. I am infected with the disease of thought.

55

Once upon a time, I carried two very drunk people to, then through, an airport. My passport did not make it unscathed. That is the only time I regretted the fact that I don't drink. Otherwise, I simply cannot understand why people do. If it is for the sake of socializing, has nobody ever been to a coffee shop?

56

People drink and do drugs. They say it's harmless or just to feel good or better. Doing *anything* because it feels good or for the sake of feeling "better" is a crime against the self. If there is a void in your soul, no pleasure will fill it. There is no substitute for love.

57

There are many things I have never done. Some would say I have missed out on life experience. I would agree. But in the end, I am myself. Part of me wishes I had experienced them. Although the same question comes back time and time again: Who would I be otherwise? Because I certainly wouldn't be me.

58

I don't even know who I am. When I dream, I don't know *what* I am. In my dreams, I have memories of being someone else. I talk to strangers like they are family. I hold memories of our time together, yet I was only just born into existence. I am *me*. I am still me. Yet I am someone else. How is that possible? This self that I am at this moment ceases to exist. Yet I am still as much myself while I am dreaming — just with no memory of *this* self. So who am I?

59

Often, I feel like I am not doing enough. There is always more I could be doing. It makes it difficult to enjoy time spent alone. Especially without friends, family, or consistent work. Spending a day inside, alone, feels like wasting my youth. But I do try. I go out, I spend time with people, I apply for jobs and work on my own.

But I can't spend each and every day — all day — doing those things. So when I am inside and alone, it feels like a waste of time. So I try to write, but I can't. I try to make art, but I can't. I try to do *something* productive, but I can't. I only consistently manage to read.

However, I have found salvation in thought. It is not wrong to be alone. It is not wrong to spend my time doing simple things to pass the time. So long as thoughts run through my mind, not a second is wasted. Perhaps I suffer for my thoughts. But does it matter if they might one day lead to happiness? Especially if they allow me to enjoy the moment.

60

I have spent my entire life traveling the world. From Antarctica to Svalbard and everything in between. What sights I have seen. What people I have met. What experiences I have had. I have traveled since the day I was born. Yet I have no desire to travel alone. I have, and I do. But I don't desire to.

The reason for that is shared experience. There is no sight in this world worth seeing alone. To me, the clouds are enough. So long as I can look to the skies, there is not a place on this earth that calls to me. Who would watch the clouds with me? Maybe someone would. Though I know many who desire to travel.

61

Such beauty as I have never before known. Within the reach of my hand is the world for which I have sought my entire life. I need only reach out, touch it, take hold. And yet it is ever out of reach. I would not dare lift a finger.

62

I don't think many people actually know what love is. If you would be annoyed by your partner, then it is not love. If you would raise your voice, then it is not love. If you would not seriously consider any and every thought, feeling, and suggestion of theirs, then it is not love.

To love someone means to love them for their flaws and to do anything for them, within reason — and for them to do the very same in return. Flaws are the important part. Someone's flaws are their expression of their ability to love. I learned that by watching a middle-aged couple argue over who sleeps where on a couch. Why argue? If you love each other, then give the spot to the other. And yet it is the fact that they

argued which demonstrated their capacity for love —
it is the bounds of emotion.

Unfortunately, *capacity* for love and love itself are
two different things. True love means dealing with
emotions maturely — not because you are mature,
but because you love your partner.

63

A girl confessed her love to me. She lied about not
having feelings for me. She thought I was lying about
not having feelings, too, because she was lying. I
thought we were friends. She thought something else.
Nothing was the same after that. That isn't love.

64

Emotions happen against our will. So does life. It
seems that every time I meet someone I care about,
one of us moves to another country. We never meet
again. After four times, the idea of a god doesn't sound
too bad. Maybe the knowledge that I am an actor in a
cosmic comedy would make it more bearable.

65

Everything that has gone wrong in my life could also
have gone right. So why did it go wrong?

66

I'll never understand how some people write. Even text messages. If I see another sequence of crying-laughing emojis or excessive abbreviation, I will never text again. Does nobody take pride in their manner of communication? Is eloquence truly lost to the 1800s? I must side with Nietzsche: how people write is indeed a sign of the times.

67

Learning the Icelandic language is a fascinating journey. In what other country do young children consider speaking English to be cool? The efforts being made to preserve Icelandic *in Iceland* are immense. But it will never be enough. Nobody wants to learn the language. I can't say I blame them — everyone here speaks perfect English, and Icelandic isn't spoken anywhere else. That, and there are no resources on par with modern language learning methodology.

My dream is to write in Icelandic. The mere thought of writing poetry in Icelandic is enough to make me *need* to write. Unfortunately, I lack the skills. If I had been studying Russian instead, I would be fluent right now. For all the effort I put into Icelandic, for all the time I have lived in this country, I have not once spoken to an Icelandic person in Icelandic.

Never before have I been so interested in a language. Never before has a language made me so sad. It is like watching an art form die before my eyes. No language is so difficult as to be impossible. None except for Icelandic. And it isn't even *that* difficult.

68

Language is a beautiful thing. Words are art. We should be proud of how we express ourselves with words. Instead, I hear slang. Is it the music? Is the rise of rap to blame? Most of my friends in the US were foreigners — a benefit of going to an international school. We all understood each other. A few months ago, I made my first American friend in quite a while. They didn't understand some things I said, such as what a "pointed question" is.

Nobody reads. In a world of social media and tailored minute-videos, who would bother to sit down with a book? That's how I learned to use words when I was a kid. I've read the work of my peers all my life. Nobody can write. Nobody can string thoughts together. Nobody has the patience to think. I question whether people are even capable of thinking anymore.

As soon as the song starts playing with talk of explicit, illicit, or unscrupulous activities, I can't help but wonder about the person playing that music. I have met only one person who reads Shakespeare, and that was not in the US. And I am no classics purist. Read anything, just not contemporary nonsense. There are good modern books. So why does everyone turn to the nonsense?

I stopped reading entirely because of school. We were forced to read books that I didn't enjoy. They weren't bad books, but I was forced to read them, so I despised reading. In fact, I cheated. I read chapter summaries, then aced all the tests and essays. Maybe if we let the students pick their own books, with supervision, the world would be a different place. If I had read Édouard Levé's *Suicide* in high school, I would be yet a different person. But how would I have ever known of its existence? That could equally be the problem: in a world where people don't read, nobody even knows what kinds of books are out there.

69

To create is to be human. And our humanity has been monetized. Social media is the bane of creativity. It's not about who is good. It's about who is popular.

70

I see the same image on repeat. People worry about AI replacing artists, especially photographers. What is it replacing? Your image of that famous mountain is just the same as the hundred thousand photographers who came before you. So what if an AI can produce yet another image of it? But that one guy is famous, so his is the best. He is worthy of his accolades. You are not.

71

So you want to write a book? You want it to be light, fun, and entertaining? Then you are welcome to *want* to write.

72

I know better than to be jealous or to judge others for their work. But some people are undeserving of their accomplishments. Art is art, yes. And what of that high schooler who pixelated black and white images of famous characters, then placed beads in a frame to match the pixels? He was given an exhibition. He made the news. Tell me he deserves the fast-track to success. Because he is in high school? If he doesn't go on to become great, then he is unworthy.

I would not care at all if only everyone else had a chance to exhibit their work. Let the unknown be known. They never got a chance. And they truly are worthy, some of them. Unfortunately, they work a 9-5.

73

Freedom is a curse. I would be happy to be told what to do. Then, when granted freedom at last, I would appreciate it *and* have a sense of direction.

74

Are the people walking down the street not your brothers and sisters? Why can I not talk to a stranger? Why do strangers not want to be talked to? We don't need to be friends, but shouldn't we at least care about one another? We are equally human with just as many problems.

75

When I receive a text message, I don't want to reply. When I do reply, it isn't me. My humanity does not translate over the internet, so I must overthink my replies only to come off too dry or too enthused. And if it didn't warrant a reply, I might simply not reply at all. Then I fear that I've done or said something wrong.

76

I am happy to talk to strangers. I speak up in groups. I put myself out there, to my own surprise. Put me in a group chat, and I'll say nothing.

77

Tomorrow is a day that will never come. I would know, I've been waiting.

78

Say yes to everything if you can. That is the fastest path to happiness.

79

Greatness is being known by a single word in the context of your work such as how Camus so casually mentions a certain type of nausea.

80

Anna Kavan's *Ice* was a strange book. It was certainly not my favorite book. It wasn't bad. It wasn't great. I have no idea what even happened in that book. But nothing else has had a greater influence on how I write.

81

I once found a stone upon which to stand. It crumbled beneath my weight. The ground upon which I landed was perfectly solid.

82

Bukowski made me a poet. Thus, he is redeemed.

83

When all else fails, move to Iceland. If you don't like it, leaving will be a success.

84

Many of the Europeans I meet dream of moving to New York or LA. Only a few have actually visited for themselves. As an American, speaking about the US with Europeans feels like we come from two very different worlds. My America is an urban hellscape where I would not dare dream of raising children. Their America is a land of hopes and dreams and boundless opportunity.

85

I know far too many girls who have been assaulted. Meanwhile, I walk down dark alleyways alone, at night. There is something very wrong with this world.

86

I used to go running with two friends. One only joined on occasion, but we would talk about all his hopes and dreams for the future. He was from China, and he wanted to build a life for himself in the US. He came in high school, that's where we met. There were a lot of Chinese exchange students.

To live in the US, however, was nearly impossible for him. So, he put together a plan where he would employ veterans to run a shooting range. All the while, he worked on himself. He must have lost a hundred pounds and replaced it all with muscle that summer. He was an interesting guy.

Sometimes we would meet on campus, and he would walk with me from building to building. He once walked around in a dinosaur costume for the fun of it. Another time, I chased him down the street because we were on the way to the theater and my friend driving suggested I go invite him to join.

I ran into him in the university dorms one day. I was going to drive my friends to get food. He asked if he could join, but unfortunately there was no room. That was the last time I saw him before he took his own life. He was 21.

87

One of my friends was assaulted by a youth pastor, a friend of hers. She attempted suicide. He walked away free and did it to another girl. He's still studying at the seminary.

88

A friend's brother got brain cancer and died. I think he was 12. I used to sit with a kid during my study hall in high school. He raced a friend on motorcycles and died. Right before graduation, one of my friends lost her dad to a drunk driver. I saw a lot of death in such a small school.

89

By the age of 24, I saw the death of four grandparents, three great aunts, a great uncle, a great great uncle, an uncle, and a friend. I've also lost four dogs and four cats. Such is the cost of life.

90

"Is there something wrong with me?" That is the worst question I have ever been asked.

91

Sitting on the beach in LA, I had a nice conversation with a friend's cousin. It was the best conversation I have ever had. We talked about art, life, and philosophy. I don't even know how long we were there. Was it 30 minutes? Three hours? I haven't the slightest idea. Nor does it matter.

92

The words we speak lose their meaning to the air through which they pass. We should hope that others understand our intentions.

93

There is no need to do anything or to be anyone. So long as you recognize your face in the mirror, you are living a good life. And if you don't recognize that face, pray it is the face of an artist.

94

Self-help will never help you. Only you can help yourself.

95

I spent most of my life in isolation. I never realized it until I was actually alone. I lived on a mountain, with no food, for over a month. That was when I finally valued other people. If I could go back in time, I would change everything about myself. All the events I chose not to go to, all the people I didn't make an effort to know. Only now do I realize my mistakes. Is it too late now?

No, it's never too late to live a life. It's never too late to do anything. But the world doesn't like late people. And we are indeed late. Childhood friends required a childhood to make. An education required youth.

Getting started in this world required help. So now we are lost and alone. What do we do?

Apart from moving to Iceland, the answer is simple: do whatever you want. It worked for me. But if you aren't at peace with being lost and alone, you will always be lost and alone.

96

Knowledge is meaningless. There is no point to knowing anything at all. Things either are or are not. What does it matter to know anything? The meaning is found in caring. That's why people talk about the weather.

97

I cry, too. In front of others. I'm not ashamed to be human. So when I ask you how you are, why do you not tell me the truth? Why do you change the topic? "The weather is good," I have heard. "I'm just busy," I have heard. But how are *you*? Why does nobody dare to answer the question? Are you ashamed of your tears? Do you feel wrong to feel bad? We may not be close, but if you don't let anyone in, then who will ever be?

98

Caring about people is easy. *Wanting* to care about someone is difficult. That is what separates "anyone" from a friend. Friends are the people you *want* to care about. But when that goes unreciprocated, what is anyone to do? Want is in short supply — in both directions.

99

I walked the streets of Reykjavík, through both residential and commercial areas. No place has such a feeling as this. It is a small town made big. The beauty of this country isn't its landscapes. Nor the city itself. It's the way life is lived. There is traffic, but no horns. The people take care of their trash. I thought I was a quiet person until I moved here, and I hardly even know any Icelanders.

Such is what it means to find a place to live. It's not about the country or the city, it's always the people. You'll never find your home until you search for it. So go out, search. If it doesn't work, go somewhere else. Change your career. Change everything. What's the point of living in this world if you aren't on a search for that which you seek?

One year ago, I was a PhD student in Salt Lake City. Since then, I have moved thousands of miles, all over the US and Iceland. I have changed careers multiple times. I have made and lost friends. I have made and left homes. I searched. And I believe I have found. What if I'm wrong? Then I will keep searching.

100

Nobody is aware of what they have because it is all they have ever known. So, leave it all behind. Try something new and different. Alone. Only then will you know what it is you actually have. Or what you even want in the first place.

101

To choose a philosophy. It is a pointless task. Existentialism? Absurdism? Nihilism? Stoicism? Some other *-ism*? The search for answers will lead only to questions. Hence, the truth is simple: if you think any philosophy will give meaning to life, you will never be happy. Because if you were happy, you would not be seeking the answers to your questions through other people's ideas.

102

What is the meaning of it all? Sometimes, I perceive signs and symbols. Once, I told a friend that I was waiting for a reply from someone else. If that other person replied, I would move forward with something. The moment I sent that message, the other person replied. So I moved forward. Another time, I had a dream come true.

Then I realized that it doesn't even matter if there is some greater meaning. The meaning isn't in the signs or the symbols — it's in the mere fact that I ascribed them meaning to begin with. So, to my chagrin, the meaning comes from *me*.

103

There was a time when I said I would rather have peace than happiness. How wrong I was to think that peace would *bring* happiness. The truth is that happiness brings peace — to everything. I am not yet happy. But I am at peace.

104

Why? That is a fun question. The answer is equally fun: Who are you? If you can answer that question, then you know your *why*.

105

I worked hard to be successful. Each accomplishment was meant to build to the next. I started when I was 16. My goal was to become a professor. I studied computer science in high school for the sake of undergrad. My undergraduate career was for the sake of doing research. My research was for the sake of grad school. Grad school was the final step. I had been offered a professorship. All I needed to do was finish.

But that was it. It truly was the last step. I had no other goals or aspirations. There was nothing else I even wanted to work towards. So why did I want to be a professor? My reasons had no grounding in reality. The closer I got, the less I enjoyed it. My professional career was decided at the age of 16. I was too young to know any better. Now I'm 25 and a starving artist. I have no complaints. I wouldn't be creating otherwise.

106

Everything happens exactly as it needs to, but only if you allow it. Resist, and you will suffer. Suffer, and you will find joy.

107

Everyone wants success to some extent. Nobody produces films to keep them private. Nobody makes art to be stored away forever. We do *desire* for our work to be seen. But *why* do you create? You must do it for yourself above all else. Because if you create for any other reason, it will show in your work. If you are not happy with it never being seen, then it will never be seen.

108

People walk loudly down the street at night. I hear their laughter. It is good to know they are enjoying themselves. A group of children board the bus. They yell and scream and laugh. They didn't even pay their fare. Both scenarios involve smiles and laughter. Both can be annoying. But only one involves happy people, so I don't mind the noise. I worry for the future of those children.

109

Modern parenting means giving your child a tablet. There are no longer parents. And there are no longer children.

110

The worst thing I have ever done in my life is rounding up my hours at a job. What I feel the most guilt for in my life is trying to care about someone who I didn't like.

111

Anyone who claims their words are important is not worth listening to.

112

The world suffers for its own suffering. Who started this vicious cycle?

113

My proudest accomplishment is making a room of diplomats cry. I spoke up because I had the chance.

I never used to speak up. Then I was alone. Now I always speak up.

114

How does one make a friend? Not just be friends, but have a *friendship*? I have made plenty of friends, but what do people do together? How does anyone spend time one-on-one? What is the process from meeting someone to developing a friendship?

I can think of one easy solution: invite that person to your own circle. Then let it all grow from there. But what does someone do when they are alone? Such is the problem of this world: circles are often closed. The circle is the barrier between *friend* and *friendship*. I once tried to build a new circle. Everyone already had their own.

115

In a world of humans, there is nothing more difficult than meeting another human. There is one person seared into my memory: the most human of us all. The only human to make me feel perfectly human. And being human isn't always a good thing.

116

There is one person I wanted to learn about because I could not understand them. I never got the chance to know them. Now my atlas of humanity shall remain incomplete for all of eternity.

117

What people do is always for a reason. Bad things, good things, it's always for a reason. We cannot judge anyone for anything they do. Not even the people who hurt us. There is a reason. We may never know or understand it. But there is *always* a reason. If we knew it, we would feel empathy rather than anger.

118

Do you feel any certain way? Other people feel that way, too. You are not alone in your feelings or your struggles. But you would never know unless you share them. I would know because I've felt the same.

119

Deep beneath the mountains of Bosnia is a tunnel system. Deep within the tunnel system is a large stone. And some French people. They sat their crystal skulls on that stone, surrounding me. They hummed and sang. They performed a ritual, and I was involved because it was a tight space with no way out. Apparently crystals only have power when they are carved into the shape of human skulls and set on ancient waterways.

120

Belief is the only powerful thing. Be it gods or crystals, nothing matters except belief. Do not pray when you can believe. Do not perform rituals when you can believe. If there is magical or spiritual power in this world, then it does not come from stone or fire. It comes from your ability to believe in that power. I don't know what I believe, and I can't say that I care. Maybe magic is possible. It makes no difference to me.

121

A man once wrote to me online. He said that he was David. My university put on a Christian play every year, I thought he confused me with another Jonathan whom I knew participated. So I asked what he meant. He said that he was David, and I was his brother, Jonathan. From the Bible.

Many years later, I heard from that man again. This time, he said he was Jesus, and that he was my dad. I wonder what leads people to such delusions. They are mentally unwell, of course. But why Jesus? That's not my first encounter with a Jesus. There is surely something much deeper-rooted in their minds than simple delusion. They could "surface" any identity — be anyone. So why Jesus?

122

I watched a show where two people did past life regressions. They had such strange yet interesting stories. I don't know whether or not I believe in past lives like that. But I was fascinated. *If* there are past lives in that sense, I was curious to know mine.

That night, I dreamt that I was looking down on myself from the sky. I was a young woman in an 1800s black dress. I watched myself go and sit on a backwards-facing seat of a horse-drawn carriage. My vision was then filled with the image of an older man with one of those curled mustaches and 1800s clothing. It was a black and white image. It was fixed in my vision for a good minute. Then I woke up.

I awoke with the knowledge that the year was 1885 and that I traveled the world with my family. We weren't rich, but we had the means to do so. Perhaps it was my subconscious creating a story for me to entertain my curiosity of past lives. Perhaps it was the truth. In either case, it doesn't matter whatsoever — I am not a woman living in the 1800s. Unless this is all a dream...

123

Reality is, in itself, unreal. If I were born blind, I would have no notion of sight. Therefore, my perception of the world would be utterly and entirely different. Other animals have other senses. They perceive the world differently. So what is the truth of this world? It could very well be a dream. I could be in cryosleep on my way to some distant star system in the year 3178. Or in the style of Alan Watts, I could be a god who got bored and decided to experience experience itself.

So what is real? I don't think it's possible to answer that question. Nor does the answer matter. I feel, though. Descartes was so close: "I feel, therefore nothing else matters."

124

True contentment is the acceptance of death. Were I told I would die tomorrow, the only thing I would do is write letters to everyone I appreciate. I suppose that means I should tell people that I appreciate them. Otherwise, I have no unfinished business. I am lucky in that way, that I create for myself. Otherwise, I should wish to be immortal.

125

What happens when I die? I don't care. I will die one day. I would like to believe in reincarnation because it sounds fun.

126

There was a time when I felt truly terrible about my existence. I wondered whether we are all better off dead. Cioran, in his infinite pessimism, was my idol: Having children? Who could ever be so cruel as to actually desire to bring another living being into this world?

Some time later, I felt joy. It was very short-lived. It was rather unfortunate. It was born and died at the hands of cruelty. I wanted to curse the name of the one who did that to me. However, in my minute of joy, I learned that life is capable of being beautiful. I learned that raising children can be a good thing so long as you are a good person living a happy life.

In fact, I would argue that this is our duty to the human race: to raise happy children. So, I thank the cruel hands that showed me life is still possible.

127

Sympathy is the most evil thing anyone can do. Have empathy, not sympathy. If you worry that you don't understand what it's like, then ask. That will gain you both compassion *and* empathy.

128

I know my friend is not happy. What do I do about it? I be open and honest about myself and my own unhappiness. It is up to my friend to open up in turn. If he chooses not to, that is on him. I did what I could.

129

For years, I bemoaned a feature I did not like. One day, I decided to fix it. I bemoan no longer.

130

I prayed one time. I wondered if God was real, and if He was, then I wanted forgiveness. So I prayed for forgiveness. Then, I realized that God would know what is in my heart — I shouldn't need to pray if He knows I am sorry. And then I realized that I don't care whether or not God forgives me. It's only how I feel about myself that matters. Thus, I rejected God.

131

The devil asks us to be happy. God asks us to suffer. It is a game of faith, and I have faith only in myself.

132

Anger is an emotion I do not comprehend. I should wish there were a god if only to strike down those who would strike others.

133

I am too old to be young and too young to be old. What does that make me? Me.

134

I hear people say how they feel exactly the same in their older age as they did in their youth. What kind of lives did those people lead? This past year, from 24 to 25, I have lived a thousand lifetimes. Each month, I became a different person. I shed my eyes and rewired my mind time and time again. At 24, I avoided people like a plague. At 25, I seek them out in fascination. It was just two years ago that I started reading again, and one year ago that I started writing.

135

Physical appearance is meaningless. Nobody cares how you look. If they do, they are fools unworthy of your time. If *you* do, you have succumbed to the plague.

136

Be healthy. Is there anything more to say about your body? You have nothing without your health. And there is nothing else about it that matters.

137

If you actively seek to be perceived as wise or intelligent, then you are neither wise nor intelligent.

138

Wisdom and intelligence are very different things. I knew many intelligent people, especially in academia. They were not all so wise. They fixed numbers and used biased techniques. It was genius. It was foolish.

139

There is an allure to the life of successful artists, musicians, actors, and the like. Is it the fame? Is it the travel? Is it the engagement? Is it the community? Be careful what you wish for.

140

Where do I go when I have seen all that this world has to offer? Home. And if I have no home?

141

To be busy is to be happy. And if you don't enjoy what makes you busy, then stop doing it.

142

Many things are easier said than done, but many people would rather talk than try.

143

People are too afraid of failure. So what if you lose your job? So what if you lose all your friends and family? So what if you lose everyone and everything you have ever known? It's better to try to be happy.

144

I went on a study tour with my university to Italy when I was 16. I went because it was my family's region. A professor invited me on a walk. I said I was too tired from the day of hiking. He said everyone else was also tired, but they were going anyway. So, I had no choice but to join. On that walk, an architecture student showed me his camera. It cost $300. I couldn't believe it was so expensive, but it was impressive — we were required to take photos for the class, and it was much better than my phone.

I bought a cheap camera when I got home. I never used it. Then I went to visit my family in Italy. I took a lot of pictures. Thankfully, I didn't know they were bad. I enjoyed it. Two years later, I bought an actual DSLR. Then I realized how bad I was. Two years after that, while studying photography, I bought a modern, mirrorless camera and lenses. I now reject the idea of photography. I am not a photographer. I do not take photos. I make art. Photography is a skill, art is something else. There's nothing wrong with photography — it *can* be art — but capturing a mere moment in time alone does not constitute art.

I learned what art is by thinking I could be a photographer. And I only became interested in photography because I went on a study tour to my family's region of Italy. Where a professor forced me to go on a walk. Was it fate?

145

Color is bothersome. How many depictions of green grass exist in this world? Unfortunately, there are no other worlds to visit where the grass is not green. So I create my own worlds. I take joy in subjecting the earth to my dreams.

146

If art is creativity, then what is more creative than inventing an entirely new artistic medium?

147

Technology has nothing to do with the problems of today's world. It is a society centered around technology which is the problem.

148

I walk alone in the dark on icy roads in freezing temperatures and blowing winds. I'm just as happy to walk as I am on a warm summer day.

149

Driving a car is evil. It's one thing to need to leave the city, but does everyone really need to drive their own car to the same place as everyone else? I ride empty buses through traffic-congested roads. Cars aren't the problem — people are.

150

The sun is out for only a few hours each day in the winter. It can be hard to get up when sunrise is at 11:30. Apart from that, each day is just like any other. Having sun all day, on the other hand, is not a good experience. I cannot write by the light of a lamp in the summer. And yet that is when I began writing...

151

I never read my book after publishing it. I don't have any desire to. I hope to forget it so I might one day read it as someone else's writing.

152

Nobody knows what they are doing. Those who appear to only seem so because they're actually doing anything at all.

153

I've met the men who rule the world. One had the waiters remove the vegetables from his plate, then replace the cooked tomatoes with raw ones. He was drunk, so I'll give him the benefit of the doubt — he paid for the dinner.

154

When I was a kid, I lived with a princess for some time. She snuck candy for my brother and I. She was just another person to me.

155

The greatest compliment I ever received was a Russian political leader telling me I was a "strong man." It meant something because he was a good person. And it was the greatest because he was Russian.

156

I bear a name that was not earned. I was born with it. And because I was born with it, I am entitled to its benefits. I would be a fool to decline them, but should I feel guilty for accepting? Life isn't fair. That wasn't my doing. So no, I will feel neither guilt nor shame. Only the determination to earn it.

157

Who are the people in my dreams that I do not know? Why do I see the same people multiple times despite not knowing them in reality? It is a sad fact that the person I am in my dreams already knows them. I would like to learn about them.

158

I once gazed into the faces of aliens. They held me in their arms as I feared for my life. Looking back, I think it was love I saw in those strange faces. Is this a true story? Am I recounting a dream? Is it a metaphor for something else? I'll let you be the judge.

159

To think we are alone in the universe is preposterous. The aliens don't make themselves known for our own protection: "Behold, a free and equal society," they would proclaim. And so the nukes would fly.

160

Gender is the most unfair circumstance in this world. As a male, I can attest that men are usually the problem. It's not a question of equality, however. It's a matter of society. There are deeper issues than gender inequality. What would drive a man to do such things? Ask his father. And his father's father. We'll find the root of the issue eventually.

161

Many things are "supposed" throughout the times. Their truth is irrelevant. If they don't hold meaning as they stand, then their validity is equally meaningless.

162

Were the moon landings faked? I couldn't care less. We have sent craft to Mars. Unless the point is to question the government. In that case, your mistake was assuming the government was ever trustworthy.

163

There is one topic I cannot write about. There is much I wish to say. The very fact that I can't write about it says more about this world than anyone will ever know.

164

I believed in science until I became a scientist. There are many undeniable truths. But once that truth becomes deniable, all hope is lost.

165

When I went to my advisor with my research plans, he said they were good. He then said there was no money to be found in that topic, so I was not allowed to pursue it. I was studying computer graphics. I wanted to research a topic related to the creation of art. I ended up researching graphics card architecture. Science follows the money, not vice versa. I quit to make art.

166

When I interviewed for PhD programs, my first-choice advisor mentioned low salaries. I told him that I didn't care about making money. He said that was nonsense, everyone cares about money. I was accepted with a special offer. I went to a different school.

167

What is the obsession with money? Everyone thinks they would be very happy to be rich. But how would your life change? Apart from actual necessity, what would be so different as to make you *happy*? The most money I have ever made was $24,000 in a year. I was perfectly rich, though I would have loved a bigger apartment. Would that apartment have made me happy, though? Absolutely not. I was miserable because of school, and I lacked the life experience to realize that I was isolating myself. Money would have changed nothing — perhaps made it worse.

168

The only thing of any value in this world is people. Good people, specifically. They are hard to find. They are repelled by bad people.

169

Why do people value fame? There are good celebrities, but even then, why value them? You are welcome to appreciate their work. But to follow their lives like a close friend? I would rather talk to my close friends. And ask about their lives.

170

I met a woman whose arm was covered in diamonds. From fingers to elbow. I have never seen so many diamonds in my life. She had terrible fashion.

171

I stumbled across a potato chip machine in the mountains of Italy. It was fully stocked. There are two ways to look at that, yet neither holds more meaning than the fact the machine exists in the first place.

172

My gut feeling has never let me down. I ignore it all the same.

173

I see other people out living their lives on social media. Sometimes, I am jealous of what they are doing. Then, I wonder why they are posting their lives on social media. For family and friends, I can understand. For the world? They must be *of* the world. I am no longer jealous.

174

I lived out of a suitcase for a year. There wasn't a thing I missed.

175

Validation. To seek it is to die.

176

There is someone I once knew who I want to sit down and have a conversation with. I will never see that person ever again. How do I reconcile that? Perhaps the only way is to meet someone else with whom I wish to sit down and converse with.

177

Tears are but the blood of an injury to the soul.

178

How do we heal from trauma? I don't think we do. I think it becomes part of us — shapes who we are. That isn't fair. We were only children. And yet we are capable of change. So we must change for the better, look back on who we were, and be happy to know that we overcame adversity.

179

There are happy people. They are rare. Most people are unhappy. Have you ever heard someone complain? I know a woman who complained about her life at home. Her son was off doing something. Her husband was doing something. The animals were doing something. They were small complaints and nitpicks. She wasn't *sad*, per se, but I don't think she was happy. To complain about anything at all must be a sign of unhappiness. Perhaps it is even subconscious.

There was a point when I wanted to ask everyone whether they were actually happy. I couldn't really believe that anyone was. That came after a rather despairing time of extreme failure and isolation. I couldn't look at anyone without imagining their unhappiness behind a mask. Hearing someone talk of struggling to pay rent brought tears to my eyes. Seeing a dirty apartment broke my heart. What would bring someone to not do the dishes?

Complaining, leaving dirty dishes in the sink, not taking out the trash, putting oneself down, talking around "how are you," changing subjects, unkempt hair, escapism. There's so much more. To me, these are signs of unhappiness. Doing the dishes isn't a chore to a happy soul.

180

I have spent most of my life around people learning English. We speak in English. They are complimented for their English. Sometimes they are happy to hear that. But sometimes they say "oh, but I forgot this," or "but I didn't do that." The same goes in many other situations with many other compliments.

Why do people do that to themselves? Why not say "thank you," and be happy for the compliment? Happiness. Self-worth. Self-esteem. There is no praise in this world that can ever change one's self-perception. If you do not value yourself, there is no such thing as a compliment.

181

If someone does something worthy of it, give them a compliment. Don't be patronizing. Mean it.

182

One of my friends expects me to say everything back. Praise loses all meaning. What she says to me, I value. What I say to her is worthless. She told me to say it. Maybe I would have on my own, but she told me to. Now it means nothing. She struggles with her confidence. I told her why I think it's a problem for her to tell me what to say. But if I don't say it, then she is hurt. What can I do?

183

I have never asked anyone what they think of me, in any capacity. I truly do not care.

184

If you hate me, I'll still invite you to coffee. Assuming I still like you. It would be a shame if you declined, but at least I tried. Just let me know so I don't bother you.

185

Am I supposed to read between the lines of your texts? Communication isn't a game. That's why I write poetry. How was I supposed to know you were secretly a poet, too?

186

If someone is complicated, they probably aren't happy. Or, they lead an interesting life. Or maybe they're an artist. Pick two.

187

Would you believe that I meant what I said and nothing more by it?

188

Someone thought I was mad at them once, because I was quiet. I can understand why they thought that, but the truth is that I had nothing to say. I was contemplating life because I met an interesting person. I couldn't believe I met an interesting person.

189

A friend introduced me to a "loud" and "outgoing" and "talkative" guy. He ended up being just some normal guy. He was a good person, I liked him. They were both Icelandic.

190

My greatest fear is being alone. Then I write. Once I start writing, my greatest fear is not being able to finish what I started. Once I finish, my greatest fear is it not being good enough. I put it out there, into the world, anyway. Then, my greatest fear is not being understood.

191

I am alone with nothing to do. That is my fear: having nothing to do. I feel unproductive. I'm not actually unproductive. And there's lots to do. But that doesn't change how I feel. I feel so unproductive, in fact, that I begin to think. And thought culminates in writing. It may take a painfully long time, but I do write in the end. Is my writing actually productive? If you're reading this, then I suppose it was.

192

I'm generally not unhappy. I'm not often happy, either. If I ever feel down, all I need to do is read. Or go for a walk. What makes me happy is spending time with others. Finding happiness alone is a challenge I am willing to undertake. If I can figure that out, I will unlock the secrets of a joyful life.

193

I intentionally limit my distractions — it makes me more productive. It's not about being productive or unproductive. But what is a distraction, and what is "spent time"? Is there even a difference? We have time to spend, so we might as well spend it. What makes something a distraction is guilt. Do you feel guilty for how you spend your time? Do you feel shame for it? Then you are either making poor use of your time, or you do not know rest.

There is no harm in being unproductive. In fact, being unproductive can lead to productivity. But mastering the art of "productive unproductivity" is anything but easy. Above all else, I simply value consistency.

194

I have many friends who enjoy social media feeds, minute-videos and whatnot. I want to ask them what they get out of it. How is that enjoyable? All those people, recording themselves doing the same things as everyone else. Who can say that one phrase with the funniest voice? Who can do that one dance in the best outfit? Who can talk over someone else's video with the most sarcasm? Those content producers are anything but funny. Some are, I will concede. And then everyone copies them, creating a platform of toxic waste.

What does anyone have to gain from consuming this media? I wondered until I went on a trip with some friends. We sat around the TV. Out came the phones and the scrolling. Here we were, my closest friends, all together after a year apart. And what do we do? Scroll. I know why. It's to fill the void. Could anyone dare to sit in silence with their own mind? Not in today's world, it seems.

There was a time when that was not an option. People had to fill the time with actual *stuff*. Like talking to friends and hanging out. Then came the internet. Now we can talk online. So talking in person isn't a priority. Then came social media. So thought isn't a priority.

195

I am harsh in my criticisms. They are deserved

196

I was born in the 1900s. I'm fortunate to have not grown up with a smartphone. When I was a kid, answering the phone disconnected the internet. When I'm old, I'll find great joy in telling everyone I was born in the 1900s.

197

Community. Where did it go? I lived in the same neighborhood for 20 years. I never met my neighbors.

I never played with any neighborhood children. The first community I ever knew was at the library here in Iceland. It's a good one, but we only meet once a week. And it's only one group.

Where is community? Can I not meet with one group on Mondays and another on Tuesdays? I would if they existed. I live in Iceland. There is no group where artists meet each week to discuss one another's work. I would enjoy that kind of community. It could only exist in this country, if nowhere else. The onus for that is on me now. I have placed a great weight upon my shoulders.

198

There was once a world where humans interacted with one another. In that world, doing anything at all meant human interaction. To the great disappointment of ever-growing corporations, humans make mistakes. They aren't very efficient. Now we talk to robots from our apartments. What marvelous technological innovations. They behave like humans, except they don't understand what we tell them. Nevertheless, they are efficient. Because if someone complains, there is not a person to blame. "It was a fault in the system."

199

When I worked as an artificial intelligence researcher, I had an existential crisis: "Is this really how my brain works?" I became self-aware of my own learning, how my brain operates by learning from predictions. "Am I nothing more than a math equation?" It's a harrowing thought.

200

I am conscious. I don't know what that means, but it's the truth. You might not be. I can't prove that I am to anyone else. But I know I am.

201

There is a housing crisis in Iceland. Rich people buy nice apartments, then put the first floor up on short-term rental sites. How many places have I stayed without decent windows? A woman on the street once locked eyes with me as I came out of my bathroom in Akureyri. I kept the curtains pulled after that. The owner of that apartment didn't give me the wifi password for four days.

202

I woke to a jingling sound, like a bell. Was it something outside? I sat up in the darkness. My curtain moved a little. I didn't have any windows open in my bedroom. "Hello?" I called, my heart racing. Then the curtains flew open. A black figure darted out at me. I screamed. It was a cat. I didn't have a cat. I threw it outside and heard the jingles every night after.

203

"No debit cards." I paid with my debit card. Nobody said anything. Do they not want money?

204

"Who are you?" a man asked me at an event. It was an Icelandic event where everyone knew each other. I was the only foreigner. "I'm Jonathan," I replied. "Who are you?" he asked again.

205

Paint? Color is my paint. That has always been my motto. I cannot outdo the work of nature. To paint is a travesty. I leave the hard work to nature.

206

I walked around a house for an hour on Snæfellsness. I photographed clouds. No place on this earth has more beautiful skies. It's a shame Iceland only has one city.

207

The romanticization of Iceland quickly gets old. Yes, the language is cool. No, it's not that cold. Yes, Icelanders are people too. They live normal lives in a normal country if you can believe that. It's still fun to talk about it though.

208

It's easy to forget that some people haven't seen much apart from their homes. I knew many Americans who have never left the US. To them, the very concept of Europe exudes adventure and romance. These are the people who visit tourist attractions and stay in hotels. I had no choice but to stay in a hotel in Iceland, once. I'll never stay at a hotel again.

209

I sat by a window with a friend. We watched a tourist walk by with a whole case of water bottles. How did we know it was a tourist? We live in Iceland.

210

I tried to buy water here. It was away from the city. I didn't bring my water bottle, and I was going hiking. The grocery store didn't sell water. There is much to be said about the society here based on that fact.

211

A hot chocolate cost five euros in Switzerland. They brought us a teacup of hot water and an instant-mix-powder packet. There is much to be said about the society there based on that fact.

212

I got distracted while taking pictures. I lost track of my group. I thought they left the historical area we were in, so I went out through the gates. It was a one-way gate. My group wasn't there. I was greeted by a sea of Tunisian taxi drivers. First, they called out in English.

I panicked and headed to where the bus had parked. Then, they called out in French. I kept walking. Then, they started yelling and cursing at me. If I wanted a ride, why did I walk *away* from the taxis?

213

How do people get by in difficult circumstances? I've heard the stories of scammers in places like India and Nigeria. "I need to feed my family," is what they often say, and they aren't wrong. So what are they to do? Are they to be blamed?

214

A Zen koan: a man was tired, so he went to sleep.

215

I read the entire works of Lobsang Rampa when I was younger. I don't know the truth of a single thing he said. Nor does it matter. I fell in love with Eastern philosophy.

216

Alan Watts was an alcoholic. He died for it. I enjoyed his lectures.

217

The beauty of the Tao is that it was written in Classical Chinese.

218

Buddhism is not a religion. Modern Buddhism is a religion.

219

When I was in high school, my Christian textbook in a religion class grossly misrepresented the idea of nirvana. It claimed that people seek to cease existing. It passively mocked the very idea in comparison to eternal bliss in heaven. I don't follow such doctrine as to have any opinions on nirvana, but I cannot stand for the misrepresentation of one doctrine to better sell another.

220

I once told a Buddhist leader from a Canadian institution that I found Buddhism because of Lobsang Rampa. He replied that the paper of Rampa's books is no better than toilet paper. That man was a leader, but he was not a Buddhist.

221

What does it matter what anyone thinks or believes so long as it doesn't impact you negatively in any way? But what if it impacts *them* in a negative way? What happens then?

222

In middle school, during Bible class, a teacher warned us of other belief systems. He was repulsed by the idea that other systems place the *self* at the center. "Nobody is above God," he pointed out. And yet what happens when my soul is lost? If I am me, experiencing the world through *my* eyes, then God is nothing more than my perception of Him. Therefore, I am more powerful than God. If God ever claims my soul, He ceases to exist along with me. That is true martyrdom.

223

I am happy to be wrong about everything I have ever believed or thought to be true. Because then I would know the truth.

224

When someone is unwilling to change their beliefs, they are not worth talking to. They don't need to change them. They just need to be willing to.

225

I met a professor who asked me why I wanted to do research. I explained, and then he said I was wrong. I don't even remember what he told me, but he made a good point. Now I enjoy it when people tell me I am wrong. If they are right, my beliefs grow stronger. If they are wrong, my beliefs grow stronger.

226

Anyone who claims to know the truth does not know the truth.

227

I'm not fond of people who don't read. Occasionally is alright, but do try to make it a habit. The decline of eloquence has an unfortunate correlation with the decline of reading. The 1800s were a magical time.

228

If you cannot communicate, you cannot succeed.

229

I understand that you have your problems. That's why I forgive you. But what of those who don't understand?

230

I know people who partook in "letting people down easy." They didn't want to be mean or rude. Instead, they were mean and rude. Nevertheless, they had kind hearts. What does that mean? It means they have great suffering ahead of them.

231

Someone asked me to do something I didn't want to do. I said no. We're friends now.

232

There was a time when I had a bad habit of checking my social media too often. I don't even use social media, so I asked myself why I was checking. The reason is that I was bored. So I stopped checking. I'm not so bored anymore.

233

My preferences for communication depend on the person. It's not a matter of what I want or my capabilities. It is simply what happens. That communication changes over time. Unsurprisingly, that change can be good or bad. But if I expect any type of change, how would the other person ever know that? So I have learned to communicate about communication. Depending on the person.

234

Understanding *why* someone communicates the way they do means everything. I'm happy to talk about the weather if I know that's your way of trying. One person used to ask strange questions. I had to repeat myself rather often. But I knew their *why*, so I was happy to do it. I knew they were paying attention.

235

"You wouldn't understand." Try me.

236

A friend confided her insecurities to me. She was wor-
ried about her appearance. I asked her if she could
think of the causes for her insecurities. She went on
to explain all the problems with her physical appearance. I didn't know what to say. I empathize. How
does one ever come to learn the relationship between
mind and body?

237

In both the US and Europe, I've met people who are
bothered by others' openness. Someone ordered a
pizza, and the guy taking the order talked about his
ex-wife. Is that strange? Probably. But maybe he just
needed to get it off his chest. That's certainly nothing
to complain about. It should be rewarded.

238

If you don't think you have any problems, then you
have a lot of problems.

239

I would tell anyone anything if they asked. It makes no difference to me what anyone knows. Maybe they can help me. Maybe I can help them. I would never know unless I'm open and honest. The hard part is having such conversations in the first place — who asks questions that require you to be open and honest? Not many people do.

But if given the chance, don't hold back. What else is the point of being human? If they think you're weird, then so be it. At least you tried. Personally, I can't say I'm very interested in that one sports match. But your life? Now that is fascinating.

240

I've never met another person who reads the same books as me. Nor have I met many people who read. That doesn't stop me from talking about books.

241

If I don't want to do something, why should I do it? If it must be done, then I'll want to do it eventually. I know this is true because I was once a scientist. Now

I'm unemployed, and I've never sold a single piece of art. All seems well to me.

242

Being whole means wanting to do the right things.

243

Everyone deserves compassion, even those who do us wrong. If you do not have compassion for them, the world will always remain broken. And I am talking about *you*. Not everyone else, but specifically *you*. Nobody else can take action. Only you can. The fate of this world is in your hands, and your hands alone.

244

I'm proud that I've changed the world. I may not have done anything, but I was born. Now the world will never be the same.

245

The people who have shaped me, made me who I am, made me an artist, made me a writer — they don't even know who they are or what they have done. Per-

haps you have shaped someone else? You would never
know.

246

Time will pass, with or without you. It would be best
if you came along.

247

People are so obsessed with moving forward that they
leave themselves behind.

248

I was taught everything from math to history in
school. The ancients taught the process of critical
thinking. I have never once needed to know the 23rd
president of the United States. I have also never needed to integrate in spherical coordinates. We study
older works because they are worthy of being studied.
What deeper meaning is there to be found in contemporary works?

That's not to say that all modern work is "bad."
Rather, minds are being wasted. We may have bril-
liant infrastructure, but what use is a modern world at
the cost of our humanity? Who will be the next Dos-
toevsky? I fear it won't even matter. When I see the list

of each month's most popular books, I am faced with sights so terrifying as to lose all hope for the future.

I was fooled, once. People claimed a certain book made them cry. They said it was such a beautifully sad story. I struggled through the first half. But the praise and the reviews kept me going. In the end, I actually did cry. I cried for the suffering I endured in reading that book.

249

My Dinner with Andre is a beautiful film. In it, nothing happens. Two people sit at a table and talk for two hours. It's one of my favorites... The crowds line up for the next superhero movie. "It was alright," they say after watching... I've never met someone who has even heard of *Aniara*... I don't blame the people, I blame the world.

250

Once upon a time, I did illegal gambling. I was 15. I turned a few cents into hundreds of dollars. The scene got shut down. I was left with assets that tripled in value over the years. That was how I learned about investing. Life experience trumps all.

251

I am no one special. I've tried to help people over the years. There's always one common problem: nobody tries. They'll put a little effort in here and there. But as soon as something goes wrong, they panic. They keep asking for help, but they stop seriously trying. Then they doubt their abilities and give up. If anything makes me special, it's the fact I don't give up. It has nothing to do with my abilities.

252

I became interested in programming when I was 12. I bought a book to learn when I was 13. I couldn't make it past the first chapter. I bought online courses, followed tutorials, and tried each and every day to learn. I never did. When I was 16, I finally had the chance to take a university course. I learned. More importantly, I learned *how* to learn.

253

My hands are outstretched before me. My feet are on the ground. There are clothes on my body. I brushed my teeth this morning. I'm seeing things, with my eyes. I hear with my ears. But it isn't me. It's just a body. I don't know who or what I am, but this body is mine.

254

The bigger questions have no answers. The truth is found only in death. Yet we are alive. So knowing what happens when we die changes nothing.

255

There is someone I think about. I don't know why they did the things they did. But it doesn't matter. I'll never know. It would be cruel of me to make assumptions. Instead, I choose forgiveness.

256

How can anyone be at peace with not knowing something? The answer is that knowledge shouldn't change anything. What you know about someone doesn't change who they are. If it does, there is a deeper issue.

257

If you are looking for anything, you are looking for a life. What does that mean if you already have one?

258

Someone tried getting to know me by asking questions: "Do you like this? Do you like that? What's your favorite this? What's your favorite that?" How meaningless that conversation was. When I tried to explain anything, I was met with "Interesting... What's your favorite this?"

259

What you like and enjoy isn't important. I care about *why* you like and enjoy those things. If you don't have a reason, you either lack a personality or an understanding of yourself.

260

To understand yourself. How is it done? By writing down all your thoughts and feelings. Then analyzing those thoughts and feelings. Then writing down your analysis. Then writing your thoughts and feelings about your analysis. Then analyzing those thoughts and feelings...

261

It is a matter of experience. *Engaging* experience. So long as thought is involved, that experience is good. I have no problem with other types of experience. However, if one is lacking in *good* experience, I can offer no remedy.

262

I have only ever been to a pub once in my life. It was empty. I got a free glass of water.

263

I imagine Greenland is a beautiful place. I've only been to a remote village. There is a lot of ice. But what kind of people would move to Greenland? It must be a truly beautiful place.

264

Where do you find others like yourself — your people? Where are your people? Go wherever you want. Wherever you find yourself, that's where they will be.

265

There are three modes of communication: talking, writing, and texting. Each one requires different skills. Today, we use only two. Not too long ago, one of those modes did not even exist. We aren't missing just a third of our linguistic capacity, we are missing half. And we are well on our way to losing the mode of speech...

266

I've known people from all over the world. I quite seriously mean nearly every country in the world. They were all exactly the same: human. We all communicated perfectly well. I can't think of one time when anyone offended anyone else, by accident, or otherwise. Because if it was an accident, they understood. So they weren't offended. I've seen many Americans get offended by other Americans.

267

The wisest of us all pass their IQ tests.

268

Many people treat their pets like children. To love a living thing is to be human. To think you know the thoughts of an animal is projection.

269

Everything you see in other people is what exists within yourself. If you are capable of true love, nobody will be capable of annoying you.

270

Where are you meant to be? What is your purpose in this world? Are you somewhere and doing something? Then that is your what and where. Even if it hurts.

271

What are we without pain? I could have lived a happy life. If I did, I would never have understood myself or others.

272

For every moment I have suffered, the joy I might find in the future grows ever greater.

273

Who do I look up to? Sadly, I must look to the ground. They are all long dead. But their words live on.

274

Who will replace the greats? There was once a world that praised artists and thinkers. Would you believe that your favorite actor did not write their own roles? Or that your favorite singer did not write their own songs? Now name a living painter.

275

Architecture is the truest of arts. To create something beautiful that serves as not just art, but as a canvas for life itself.

276

We have replaced art with technology. No, AI will not replace any real artists any time soon. But AI *is* art. And who do you know who has created an AI that creates art? We have finally corporatized art itself.

277

The world suffers from misunderstanding. It's everything from the news to the ways in which people learn things. I can understand why someone who doesn't understand the workings of AI might find it difficult to learn its true nature. But if you wish to make any claims, you must first try it for yourself. AI has vast knowledge, but no creativity. It cannot feel. So, if your work comes from a feeling, then you are safe. Try it out. You will see... Unless you are reading this from the future.

278

I hope that AI replaces all our jobs. I long for the day when we are finally free to pursue our desires with no obligations whatsoever. The difficult part of reaching that stage will be overcoming corporations trying to monetize our uselessness. First will be entertainment. Then people will get bored. Perhaps virtual reality will come next — with virtual jobs. Then people will get bored. It will be a war against boredom that ends in revolution. And then we will be free. Or, the earth will be destroyed. In either case, we get freedom in the end.

279

Why is the "best" job to be a doctor? I have many friends in medical school. I know doctors. They're just normal people, no more worthy of respect than anyone else. But their job "helps" people. And makes a lot of money. Therefore, it is the best job. Like everything, people can be both good and bad. Good people, bad people, good doctors, bad doctors. All exist. What even *is* a doctor, though? Is it a person, or is it a job? That depends on the doctor.

280

I ran out of options — out of things I wanted to do, anyway. I tried my best. I failed. What else was there for me to do? Join the military. The Space Force looked interesting. I seriously considered it. They would send me to officer school. I would be able to put myself to use somewhere, hopefully doing something useful and interesting. Did I want to do that? Not really. I wanted to go back in time and study psychology.

There was a job listing for plumbers. They would train interested people and pay them to learn. What else? If I wanted to be a psychologist, why not let me learn what a psychologist actually does? Let me study in the field. Let me work in the field. Let me obtain a *practical* education. And do not punish me with debt. I'll gladly do it for free. I will *work for free*. Because I get an education out of it.

Surely I have demonstrated my abilities to be a good student. Sadly, to change careers in this world is impossible. You can always go back to school, but only if you have the time and money. And a lot of patience. All I wanted was to start a life. What would the world look like if we had a "scientific military"? Instead of training people how to kill, we train them to do science. Or better yet, we work together. As a world. And let humans participate in the society in which they live.

281

Have you ever killed someone? The internet loves murder. Let's say country X is the "good guy" and country Y is the "bad guy." They are at war. A soldier from X kills twelve soldiers from Y. He is praised as a war hero, celebrated, and the internet cheers. Meanwhile, those twelve soldiers were drafted against their will. They had wives and children, families that relied on them. But who cares. They were from Y. So they obviously deserved it. As did their families...

Not everyone has a choice. You are no better than a murderer if you would pick a side other than peace in a war. So what if Y was the aggressor? That does not make each and every citizen of Y a bad person. Nor does that make each and every citizen of X a good person. Who is to blame, then? Who should we focus our rage upon? The leaders. They are the only people to blame. It's their war, not the people's. They are the truly evil ones.

282

I often wonder whether the things I do are right or wrong. I try my best, but I wonder if my best isn't good enough. It's hard to accept that I might never know. But I should take solace in the fact that I bothered to wonder.

283

I feel a great amount of pressure to be somebody I'm not: to be outgoing, funny, engaging. To command attention. But that isn't who I am. So why do I feel that pressure?

284

Nothing needs to be serious. That doesn't make anything any easier.

285

Hope is what separates a good day from a bad day. Hope is fleeting. Is it wrong to cling onto it? To not let it go? What about thoughts, visions, ideas? Memories?

286

I went somewhere where I had a good memory. What happened that I returned to that place with a bad memory? The memory itself is still good...

287

To want to forget. As much as we might want to, it cannot be worth it.

288

Why is it that good memories are so difficult to recall? I spent time with someone which I enjoyed. But when I think of them, only negative memories surface.

289

I had a very good friend. They left a lasting impression on me. It was my first time being inspired by the mere presence of another person. They made me understand that being a good person means inspiring others simply by being yourself. The last thing I ever heard from them was that we would talk later. They left without saying goodbye. I never saw them again.

290

I said goodbye to someone, once. They didn't say it back. I never saw that person ever again. That wasn't their first time not doing something. Their inaction made me a writer. By doing literally nothing, they changed my life.

291

If I could tell the people who impacted me what exactly they did for me, I'm not sure they would be so happy to know.

292

So many people come and go. Why can't they stay? Apart from the fact I went to an international school. After that, I was the one who left.

293

In the darkness, I walked alone. In pouring rain, I was soaked. Streets of ice. Unrelenting cold. No signs of life around me. I didn't even know where I was going. I had never been there before. For nearly an hour, I trudged onwards. I got a haircut. I didn't want to take the bus.

294

I watch the people below move about their lives. Who are they? I'll never know. I know nothing other than the brief glimpse I am granted from my window as they walk away, out of my sight. Do they see me here, looking out my window? Do they ever look up and wonder who it is that resides in that building over-shadowing them? When I live on higher floors, what happens below seems so far away, so distant.

295

Are other people just as lost as I am? Since just last year, I have moved nine times. I move again next month. Also since last year, I have traveled all across the US and Europe. I've also changed careers multiple times in that year. I've done so many things and met so many people. Yet here I am, drifting. I'm only now starting to find my footing after 25 years in this world.

296

To go against everyone and everything, that is what I live for. That is why I value being different above being good. I will never be the best at anything. But I can be the first.

297

My determination is to live. I shall live before I die.

298

If I do not care about you, then who will ever care about me?

299

To practice what I preach. I try. Just because I know what I need to do doesn't mean I have reached that point yet. And that is perfectly fine.

300

Who can outdream God? Man.

301

Lics can be more revealing than the truth. But tell the truth anyway.

302

Have I ever mentioned that I live in Iceland? It's a nice place. I came here with a dream. That dream didn't work out. Because of that, I learned that it doesn't matter where I live. I could live anywhere in this world, and it would be exactly the same. I would still be me. It's a good thing I realized that *after* I moved to Iceland.

303

The only thing I ever wanted to do in life is make the world a better place. I thought I could become a professor and inspire students to pursue their dreams and enjoy the process. I thought programming was fun because it was like solving a puzzle — I wanted to share my joy. Then I learned what the world was really like.

304

In undergrad, the science building had large double doors. They were closed between the departments. After class, everyone would stream out, heading towards the exit behind those double doors. Everyone walked out the left side — the side close to the stairs. It was always congested. So, I would walk past everyone, open up the right side, and go about my day. I never understood why nobody bothered to open that other door.

305

How well do you really know anyone? You won't know anyone unless you give them a chance.

306

Never give up on anyone. Such is your duty. Sadly, there is only so much we can do.

307

How do I convince someone to care? How do I make someone want to be a good person? How do I show someone they are wrong in their ways? I don't know.

308

I once produced an award-winning film. It was the final project in a math class. It actually did rather well, going on to be referenced by a famous channel. I don't know how that happened. As much as I wish it were possible, no deeper message can be conveyed in a math video. I guess it was educational, though.

309

The last time I did any actual math was when I was studying math. I only did that to get into grad school. I don't remember anything from it. That shows the importance of actually caring about things. I would add that it also points out a major flaw in the educational system.

310

I feel like a pretentious narcissist when I mention anything I have done. But I enjoy hearing about what other people have done. I can't be in the wrong for talking about my own life, can I?

311

Do I really have anything of value to say? Do my words really hold any importance? If I were an old man, maybe I would be proud to say "yes, they do." But I'm not ready to be an old man. For now, I guess it doesn't really matter — it's not for me to decide.

312

Someone, somewhere, is looking out their window, wondering: "Is there anyone else, anywhere else, looking out their window, wondering if someone else, somewhere else, is looking out their window...?"

313

Different types of speech suit different types of people. But in the end, all we seek is understanding. What if you don't understand what I say? What if I don't understand what you say? We are different people with different manners of speech. That should never make a difference. Unless literal meaning is lost, speak as you see fit. If eyes are the window to the soul, speech is the window to the mind. Let that window be clear.

314

I have bled. I have wept. My canvas is painted.

315

For all I have learned about life, I know nothing about living.

316

Can someone take my hand and guide me — teach me, show me the way? But who would? And why would they? What would I even want to learn? Where does anyone begin without knowing what questions to ask? I want to learn nonetheless.

317

I've been trying to say something my entire life. I still don't know what that is. I imagine that if I keep writing, I'll say it eventually. Will I know when I do?

318

Whither, whence, thither, thence, hither, hence, and so on. The simplification of language is unfortunate. There is a charm lost to time. I can't use those words because I missed that charming time period.

319

I enjoy Icelandic because I don't need to know Greek, Latin, French, German, or Old English just to know what a word means. Although I can't say that knowing the words "flood-horse" or "tall-man" are particularly helpful. "Zebra-horse" is self-explanatory, though.

320

"To be, or not to be?" Not in Russian. That's a layered one.

321

Konglish is a fun linguistic development. Icelandic is the anti-Korean. And as much as I love Icelandic grammar for its poetic capacity, Korean grammar puts every other language to shame.

322

Learning a second, *unrelated* language should be a requirement in every school in every country. I learned more about English by studying Russian than I ever did in school.

323

The best English speakers I know are foreigners; their grammar is perfect, and their vocabulary is wonderful. "I seen," "ain't," "that's not no good," and so on. I shouldn't complain about colloquialisms, but I will stand by my belief that eloquence is a virtue until the day I die. Then there's the topic of slang...

324

Orwell had some right ideas about language and society. It's a shame Julia came from that same mind.

325

The indefatigable Huxley had interesting ideas. His delivery was rather odd, including indefatigable descriptions of his characters by the shape of their skulls. That was not so indefatigable.

326

Zamyatin often gets lost in the mix. How many authors have been lost entirely? Especially in the past, when self-publishing didn't exist? There must be countless authors who, if discovered, would redefine literature as we know it. Whose manuscript, now yellowed and tucked away in an attic, could have changed the world? We also face yet a different problem today: What is lost to the sea of self-published books?

327

I spent my lifetime breaking down the walls of this room within which I am trapped. At last, I poked a hole. And outside, there was nothing.

328

The world is nothing but a play, and I forgot my lines.

329

Each passing moment, a stranger is left in my stead. The man I once knew is lost to the past. In the time it takes me to wonder who it is I have now become, I am become someone new.

330

If I can understand myself, I can understand the world.

331

If you placed a mirror before the pages you read, you would be reading the same book.

332

I paint a self-portrait because painting is a form of art. I am not a painter. Yet here is my portrait.

333

"Just one more," I said. It never came. "I'm tired," I said. So I wrote it down.

334

I write by not writing. The more I don't write, the more I write.

335

The greats were not always great writers. And yet they wrote. And yet they are great.

336

Will anything ever be enough? No. And if that is not enough, nothing will ever be enough.

337

I don't want to be great, I want to be understood.

338

I'll never know if I'm actually understanding some-one without having them there to tell me I under-stood correctly.

339

I struggle alone because the people surrounding me are struggling alone.

340

Why is it so difficult for people to be kind, com-passionate, caring, and understanding of one anoth-er? Why are people so quick to place blame on oth-ers? Or not acknowledge, let alone realize, their own faults? The sad reality *is* reality. As in, *their* reality — they have not experienced others being or doing those things. Very few people have, in a healthy way. And it goes beyond these attributes.

The way we think, act, and react. It's all according to what we have seen and know. When somebody communicates in a way we don't understand, to *them*, it makes perfect sense. To *us*, it cannot be deciphered. In the same way, what we do can just as easily be lost to others simply because they lack the tools to understand. There is nothing to blame but the world.

341

I fear the outcome of an event that has yet to happen. Therefore, I feel anxiety. But if I have not acted, what do I fear? The only thing standing between the event and its outcome is myself.

342

Take everything at face value unless given cause to take it otherwise. Do not fall victim to your mind.

343

There is nothing worse than fear. The opposite of fear is action. The worst anyone can say is "no," and yet that "no" has the power to end life as we know it.

344

Waiting. If not for Godot, then for what?

345

If waiting is consciously on your mind, then you are not doing enough at that moment.

346

How unoriginal must one be to be originally unoriginal?

347

There was someone I quite enjoyed interacting with. One day, I couldn't understand what happened. They simply stopped making sense. Their tone changed. Their attitude changed. I couldn't tell if it was passive aggression or "plausibly-deniable" rudeness. We interacted again some time later, by chance. It was as though nothing had happened. To my surprise, that's because nothing had happened. My mind was taunting itself.

348

The only waste of time is wondering whether you've wasted your time. But if you conclude that you haven't wasted your time, then it wasn't a waste of time.

349

Anything you fear to lose is not worth having. Nor would it benefit you to have.

350

You can't truly know someone unless you love them unconditionally.

351

Why must we suffer to grow? Is it really just not possible to learn and grow *without* suffering?

352

Schopenhauer, like all who become disillusioned to the world, sought only one thing: not philosophy, but humans.

353

I know that which might heal my wounded soul. And yet that is but a dream. But what is life if not a dream?

Are they not one and the same, or is that the cost of our existence: that our dreams be but dreams?

354

A lifetime of suffering brings value to simplicity.

355

My New Year's resolution was to reach out more to people. Come New Years, those people reached out to me. I guess there's only so much I can do.

356

There is a person who I cannot understand. The more I learn about them, the less I understand. The more I try to understand them, the less I understand. This person also happens to be the only person I truly seek to understand. Could it be that people are actually difficult to understand? Or is there something I'm just not understanding?

357

My mind creates stories. It envisions all possible reasons for which someone might do something. It chooses the worst of those reasons to craft a story in which a good situation is actually bad. Or an unsure situation is actually bad. Or a bad situation is even worse. It is entirely possible. These stories are based on reality. I have only my memories. My mind paints them poorly.

So how do I know the truth? How do I escape this cycle of self-defeatism? How do I gain a grasp of my own mind? Unfortunately, I do not know. However, I can accept that these are nothing but stories — just as likely as the good stories I can spin for myself. Then, I can choose to remember a very important fact: I don't actually know the truth. Nor does it matter.

358

By some miracle, I have surrounded myself with people who understand me and accept me for my flaws. Perhaps that is because I am accepting of other people's flaws.

359

I compare myself to others and always feel the worse for it. There are aspects of myself I do not like. And yet I like those very aspects when I see them in other people. Still, I wish to be like yet others. To my surprise, others like those same aspects of me. Either that, or it's all an elaborate ruse based on pity because they feel sorry for me. Oh mind, what a wondrously terrible thing you are.

360

Good things happen whenever I write. It's rather peculiar. I never can write when I want to. But I'm often waiting or hoping for something. When, at long last, the writing begins, other things start happening. It happens every time. Always good things. I should hope to never stop, but those very things distract me from my writing.

361

I would say what I have to say because I have something to say. If I did not say it, I would not be human.

362

Darkness seeps and fills the cracks. Lights dim as shadows close. Silence puts an end to thought. Cold draws strength from what was heat. And what remains? Who is left? In this cold, dark abyss? Whatever enters shall shine a light so bright and warm as to fill this empty space.

363

And yet it is empty. And yet there is nothing. And yet there is no one. And yet the world is so very full.

364

What do I fear to miss by making use of my hands? For what does the world go on whilst I am busy? For what do my own hands labor? Were I to sit alone with time, it would be no enemy. Yet I am never alone.

365

To show someone. For them to see. Why do they not ask questions? Would I ask questions? It isn't that I hoped. Rather, I dreamt.

366

Rhyme, rhythm, and cadence. These are the heart of poetry. And yet to read a poem without knowledge of the author's voice is to compose a piece of your own. Hope that you and the author are both poets.

367

Depressed and pessimistic literature is fascinating. I find nothing to be gained in reading about joyous lives and the beauty of the world. In sorrow and suffering alone is beauty to be found. By standing upon the heights of despair, I gaze down upon a wondrous, beautiful world. Were I to hear only of the joys of life, in no way would the passing clouds cast light upon a darkened earth. Were I to hear only of others' happiness, in no way would the simplicity of being bring peace unto my soul.

368

It seems that all has led me here. That for each choice I made to end in regret. That for each action I have made in failure. That for each word I have uttered in error. That for each step I have taken in the wrong direction. That for who I was in all my flaws. It has all led to this moment.

369

And what has led you here, to this moment? What action did you take that changed the course of your life? Not because you wanted it to. Not because you planned for it to. But because life took a course of its own. I wanted to take a class when I was 16. I wasn't allowed to. My teacher denied me the ability. I was forced to take a different class. That class required me to volunteer. The person I chose to volunteer for set me on a path that leads to where I am now. All because I wasn't allowed to take a class when I was 16.

370

Is there a reason? Is there a purpose? The same questions, again and again. There must be. But why must I be human? Why can I not learn some other way? What is my role in this cosmic reality? What point is there to learning? What point is there to existing? If there is any reason to exist, is it not to be happy? So why are we not happy? What is the reason for that?

371

The pursuit of our desires: that is our human duty. To have good desires: that is our humanity.

372

The best things that ever happen to us are the worst things that ever happen to us.

373

To whom do I owe everything? If not the muse, then there is nothing to be owed.

374

I drove through Indiana, through seas and seas of corporate buildings and campuses. Overpasses, parking lots, and massive buildings. All brand new or actively being built. The closest city to my hometown is in Indiana. Every available square foot was purchased by a real estate giant. In my home region of Michigan, every existing medical facility was purchased by a medical giant and conglomerated. These are but small examples close to home.

Each and every penny earned is being paid to a corporation. Good luck finding a better job, they own all the jobs. This is the death of the world. There are a few people sitting on gilded thrones. They are the citizens of this world, not you. Thus, there is no hope. Am I to compete with an army of kings? Dare I speak up when desperation leaves a sea of replacements in my wake?

If we wish for a future, what can we do? I lack the power to change the world. I alone cannot fix things. But perhaps I can speak up. Perhaps others will listen. Perhaps others will speak up. Perhaps others still will listen. And because I spoke up, the world might one day be changed. Because you listened. And because you spoke up, too.

375

Partying. Drinking and partying. Drugs and raves. People want to have fun. People are allowed to have fun. But *why* do they find certain things to be fun? What kind of crowd is attracted to the same events? What kind of people participate in the same activities? Surely there is common ground — some common factor bringing these people together. There are great insights about the state of our humanity to be found in identifying these threads.

376

Is the very idea of "human" to be found by averaging together the minds of all humans? Are we able to separate the "self" from the human mind? Beneath it all, who are we? Does the mind dictate the body, or does the body dictate the mind? Or is there even a difference? I have tried to be logical and rational about emotion. And yet emotion is neither logical nor rational. As much as I might understand the cause of a feeling, there is no amount of thought in the world that can change that feeling.

377

If the purpose of life is to learn and to grow, then will I ever be afforded the chance to put my learning and growth into practice? Would there be any point otherwise?

378

Responsibility. How hard could it be? If you want to do something, then do it. So why can't we?

379

In my search for answers, I have found no answers. I have gained no knowledge. Perhaps that is wisdom. Would I be a fool to say I have gained wisdom?

380

I wasn't sure what to do in a situation. So I did what *I* wanted to do. It worked out.

381

There is nothing wrong with silence. There is no point in saying something when you have nothing to say.

If you never have anything to say, there is another problem.

382

I hear the wails from the heavens: the lamentations of humanity. Each face is etched with poetry. Each voice layered with song. From the skies come harmonious symphonies, playing with the reading of the soul. No drop of rain is not a tear. No ray of light is not a reaching hand. "Behold," they cry out between cracks of thunder as leaves are blown throughout the air, "you who weep at night, do you look not to the sky?" And so, lightning strikes, catching fire to the world. The echoing wailing ceaselessly sounding, life forms withering like pages crumbling. "Dare you not," they proclaim through the shuddering of the earth, "to look your fellow man in the eyes and allow but a single tear to speak what all your words could not?" And they wept. And man did not.

383

They go about their day. But the day is not theirs.

384

Who would set fire to this earth — that it be cleansed or scorched; redeemed.

385

Were there a god capable of emotion, it would weep at the sight of humanity. Were it responsible for its creation, it would weep for the suffering it has wrought. And what is a god to do when its creation runs awry? Weep. Lest it walk amongst men.

386

For what do you seek the input of others? For what do you share yourself with the world? What is it that you seek? What is it that you go without? Do you take no pride in who you are? Do you find no solace in your reflection? Must the world be your mirror? Must they dictate your perception of self? I have seen you. I have known you. I know that you are good. Is that not enough? Because the world is blind.

387

Death is your salvation. You shall know no end to suffering. And yet you must live. So live; live that you might know joy.

388

I cannot remember your face. Try as I might, you are gone. Though we only just met. Are you a figment of my mind? Is your character of reality? From where comes your perfection — that you be but only human? And human, you are. And so, you are perfect.

389

I waited. I acted. I searched. I sought. I listened. I learned. And who did these things? It could not be me, for I am lost.

390

I will not wait for you. I shall stand by your side until the day bids us part. And when I go, I shall not look back. I asked for you to join me. You are welcome to walk alone.

391

Winds shall blow, but not me over. Rains shall fall, but not me down. I stand in opposition to nature. Whose order is to lay all to rest.

392

To exist. Such is the cosmic act of indignation. Life fighting death. Being fighting nonbeing. And what does it mean to not be? So the greats have asked. Who were we before our birth? Who so dared to incite the wrath of existence? Who, in their state of nonbeing, wrought existence itself? I ask not "*What* am I?" I ask, "*How* am I?"

393

I drifted down the river, pulled along by its current. Did I not see the reaching hands? Did I not reach my own? For how long have I drifted? And for what did I not take hold?

394

It was never a matter of asking questions. It was simply a matter of wanting to know. Of taking interest. Of being curious. That in your eyes is my reflection.

395

I sailed so far to behold the color green. To find life in a world long dead. And there, at long last, I beheld it. Then, did I know warmth. And then, I sought to hold it. Then, was I alone. No different than before. But now without direction.

396

Where would you go, if you were free? What would you do, if you could choose? No thought you might hold can hold against fate. No greater greatness is there to be found. No lower lows are there to be seen. It is not a choice. And that is what gives it meaning.

397

What have I to be proud of? I have done only my diligence. So fate commands me — my actions are not my own. And so I take no pride. Rather, I take joy. I take joy in knowing that I have acted. Even if the act brings me no joy.

398

Philosophy is nothing but wasted thought. No words can bring meaning to a life. No beliefs can bring life to the unliving. Only action has power to accomplish. Agree. Disagree. It changes nothing. Live. Die. The choice is yours.

399

How does anyone learn how to live? First, by being unhappy. Then, by trying to be happy.

400

If you're unhappy, it's because you drove to work instead of walking. And if you're unable to walk to work...

401

What if we don't know what to do, or how to do it? Then you are caught in the trap of looking for answers.

402

I'm simply trying to understand who I am and what it means to be human.

An Afterthought

0

In the process of not publishing this book, of course, much changed. So I must share my thoughts and feelings after having shared my thoughts and feelings. What a surprise that life had plans in store, that nothing would go as planned itself. Yet here I am, remaining — holding on to the remaining thread of thought before the rift between who I was and who I am is seen from the bottom.

In a way, I've done nothing in the five months between writing this book and these afterthoughts. But in a way, that "nothingness" is everything. I moved. I got a job. I met people. I lost people. I gained hope, I lost hope. And in the end, I found nothing. And that is the beauty of it all: nothing. Nothing at all. That was the key all along:

that there is *nothing. There never* was *anything. There was only ever me. And that is what I have found — though I am lost.*

1

It was neither the whisper of the wind nor the patter of the rain. It was me and I: that I should seek to listen to that which makes no sound, search for patterns in the chaos that is nature. Now is only my breath. And such is my silence.

2

It turns out that I was wrong. And until I knew that I was wrong, I thought that I was right. Or, rather, I didn't know. I was never really sure. But now I know. And now it is too late. To be wrong is never easy. To acknowledge mistakes is always hard. But now I know. But I know not what now.

3

No, it was not my fault. Nor anyone else's. It is merely the way of things: that through experience, we grow. I ask why that experience must be painful. Alas, there is no answer. So I turn to myself, the depths of my mind; and in my understanding of myself I find understanding of the world. This is my world. Yours is yours. I cannot experience what is not me. I cannot know what I cannot be. Only by knowing myself can I learn to accept the role I play in my life. And the impact that self has on others. If you are not honest, however, I will never know. So be clear; be honest. Be heard. You'll never know who is listening. If you don't speak, you will never be known.

4

It is time for whatever comes next. And what comes next? If I knew, I would not be alive. What if I am not living?

5

Prose say what words cannot. Words are meaning-less.

6

The moral high ground is the lowest ground. And blame, the sharpest sword. The only fault is ever yours. How terrible responsibility is.

7

The power I gave you over me was my vulnerability: that I trusted you, because the weight of the world is too much to bear alone. And you dropped it. The joy of a shattered world is the relief of its weight.

8

It is not foolish to be a fool. It is human.

9

The pain of written words is revealing the inner thoughts of others. What it says when my words have two interpretations and they reach the wrong one.

10

I have no patience for escapism. If you want to escape, you are welcome to. I will go my own way, and I will not stop going until I am out. Even if I never escape.

11

Of all the things I have learned, the greatest lesson I have learned is that it is never too late to learn.

12

I met an old man. We bonded over a passion for the intricacies of society and language. We started meeting weekly. He likes to talk. It's good that I like to listen. We don't exchange any contact information, only "Does this day work for you next?" And that is all. It feels so very human. When we last met, we talked for six hours. When I went home, I realized the day was over — it vanished. Positively. The next day, a colleague asked what I did yesterday. "On Sunday? I worked," I told her. "Today is Tuesday," she said.

That entire day disappeared from my mind. The very concept of time "stopped." I said something during our conversation that captures the discussion I found so interesting: "As life is made easier for us, the quality of that life decreases." This man told me about his experiences as a kid, turning a sheep's jaw bone into a toy horse by wrapping it in grass — compared to buying a toy off the shelf these days. We talked a lot about linguistics, like how modern language is nothing but direct simplifications. The depth of "flowery language" is lost because we see it as flowery. Read a book from the 1800s, like *Jane Eyre*. Maybe the story isn't life-changing, but the pure expressiveness of the language *is*.

Hence my love of prose: to say so many things without needing to say them. Then, others' interpretations fill in the gaps. Their very understanding of the words is their very self. I told someone I considered a very good friend that they needed to do some self-reflection. It was a harsh thing to say, but it needed to be said harshly in that situation. They responded by ending the friendship. "You can keep your poor opinions about me if that is to your comfort," they said. But I never once thought poorly of this person. In fact, I outright told them how highly I thought of them not too long before. Thus, my understanding is that this person has a poor opinion of themself.

I could be wrong, but I don't think so. They did tell me such personal thoughts before, anyway. It is simply fascinating, how self-perception and worldviews color understanding and interpretation. My afterthought is this: people pour out their souls in every possible thing they do. Every word they speak, every article of clothing, every motion of their body, even the movements of their eyes. That is what makes it possible to "pick up on someone's energy." It is those subtle cues that cannot be avoided.

The clearest expressions are those spoken vaguely. I worked briefly with a girl who expressed her liking of Frankenstein's monster, saying how he was misunderstood. One or two sentences, that's all it takes. She poured out her heart and soul with that expression. But who was listening?

13

In my Icelandic studies, I've learned quite a lot about Halldór Laxness. Specifically, people saying how they don't want to read his work because it is sad and depressing. Meanwhile, my coworkers started a reading club. It's fantasy romance with the likes of enemies falling in love with one another because they are bonded to their dragons who happen to be mates, so obviously the enemies must feel what the dragons are feeling and fall in love because their dragons are in love. I'm not going to comment on that. Rather, I will notice the avoidance of Laxness and the attraction to romance stories.

There is depth to life. And life is difficult. There is so much to be learned through pain, grief, and hardship. Is there much to be learned from mating dragons? Fun is allowed, but growth is essential. I think many people fear growth. They fear to leave their comfort zones — their mental comfort zones. They fear self-reflection. They fear looking into themselves and seeing something they don't like. They fear the sadness that comes with the realization that they are fundamentally broken. They fear the action, the insurmountable action, required to put their life back in order. Hiding from darkness does not constitute light.

I can understand how people might read my writing and say that I am assuming everyone is secretly miserable. That isn't the point. The point is that there is work to be done, and nobody wants to do that work. Most people aren't even aware of that work. That doesn't mean they are necessarily miserable. Rather, it means they are not happy. All I say is that happiness is our utmost goal. There is no other reason to exist. It is the essence of our humanity: emotion. We don't need to actually be happy. Not even once. We only need to try to be. That gives life its meaning.

This is exemplified by my experience with the Icelandic language. I've been in Iceland for six months. I learned to speak Icelandic. Apart from a handful of people who have lived here for years, I'm the only foreigner I know who actually speaks Icelandic. Obviously, I don't speak fluently, but I chose to move to Iceland. It is my responsibility to learn the language of the very country in which I live: I chose to take responsibility. The very same way I chose to take responsibility for my life by giving up every comfort I have ever known to build this life here for myself. Therefore, when I say others are *not* taking responsibility, I mean they are exchanging glances while waiting for instructions that shall never come.

Do I know what I'm doing? Am I good at it? Am I the authoritative voice on action? Do I know what truly leads to happiness? Do I follow each and every instruction I give to others? No. Not at all. In fact, I have nothing to back a single word that I write. Nor do I care. I had a great day today. I was responsible for that, inviting people to spend time together. What more credibility must I have? I didn't have many great days in the US. Then I changed my life, and now I do. I'm responsible for that.

14

I am driven to live not because I want to live, but because I am alive. I seek life.

15

I am saddened by recent events which often leave me feeling hopeless or that my efforts are pointless. I long and long for life. Then I realize: this *is* life. There is nothing more. The only thing that exists to change is me. Does this change the events which leave me saddened? Does this bring me hope and meaning? No. But they change me.

16

I desire to write, so I do, I will. Nothing I write will ever be good enough — because writing cannot express what is felt, I cannot transfer my consciousness using mere words. That is what makes writing meaningful to me: I can spend the rest of my lifetime attempting to convey this feeling, and I will never succeed. I am therefore allotted an entire lifetime to write. Is that not fascinating in and of itself?

17

I have yet to meet another person who writes. Photographers, painters, directors, singers, dancers, illustrators, linguists, etc. But none who write. Many do read, however. I'm not entirely sure what to make of that.

18

I thought about moving to Finland. Perhaps I one day may. But I also thought about what I might find there. Here I am, in Iceland. In the six months I have lived here, I have built a life. Not the life I yet want, but *a* life. I came here with nothing. So why Finland? Why elsewhere? In my mind, it is the idea of seeking: that I want something, and it is my duty to find it. However, I do not know what that something is. I can search near and far — what is the point?

If nothing changes, will I be able to stay in Iceland? If I am being honest with myself, probably not. Perhaps that is why I look for something new. People come here. People go here. Already, many of the people I came to call friends have left. More are leaving. *All* of them are leaving, all but one, actually. And that is not even an exaggeration. Perhaps my search is for permanence. I want something permanent. Such is one of life's banes: nothing ever is. All that is left to do is write and make art. The only certainty I will ever have is the work of my own hands. In Iceland. In Finland. In the US. If I can find some consistency, I might learn to cultivate permanence.

Regardless, I believe part of the issue is this: I live in Iceland. I know more Fins than I know Icelanders. I know two Fins. They left. Of course, I am referring to *að þekkja*. I truly wish that were not such a difficult word to use here.

19

I looked once to the color green, that a crown gilt should shine a light. But green has faded now to grey, brown now set upon the head. What was regal walks now among. Pride fallen as tears. Words I now under-

stand. I reached a hand, and it was taken. For a fallen
soul to pull. Up it rose and down I went. Where green
now fades to grey.

20

Nú breytist vor, að sumri förumst. En hvað þýðir
breyting? Þegar við erum aðeins það sem nær? Nær
hverju? Nær til hvers? Sólin lýsir okkur með ljósinu
sínu. Sólin lýsir okkur með röddunni sinni. Svo förum
við. Til þar sem er í myrkrinu enn.

21

Þetta reddast. Þangað til það gerist ekki. Þá erum við
ein. Þá erum við glötuð. Aðeins þá erum við heil.

Gods weep not for mortal men. For gods know no men are mortal. Yet when mortality faces men, men weep for those who are mortal. But I am not the one in flesh. Nor men that yet lay still. Who we are is all we're not. And we are not of flesh.

Be this world through human lens, I am I who sees. Be these thoughts in human tongue, I am I who thinks. I am I who sits behind. I am I who feels. The time that passes is but my expression. For I cannot be without time.

The gods who watch us from above look down on us with pity. To them to whom time matters not, no time is there to pass. But gods feel not emotion. Such is the eye who sees.

So what is man to do? When mortals are to weep? When time is that which passes? When I am I who sees? I cannot know my future. Nor the purpose of my past. The present is forever. In the present I do weep.

Knowing joy does not end tears. Nor does understanding. The gods that themselves know what joy should bring do not themselves know joy. Nor do they weep. For the tears we shed are of our flesh. And our joy is being man.

About the Author

Jonathan Swerdlow grew up in an international community where he was exposed to individuals from all worldly backgrounds. Additionally, he spent most of his life traveling the world, engaging in eclectic activities including sailing to Antarctica, studying religion in Turkey and Tunisia, and accidentally participating in a crystal skull ritual in underground tunnels deep beneath the mountains of Bosnia.

Jonathan has a formal education in computer science, mathematics, and photography. For most of his life, he worked as an academic researcher, giving talks and lectures in addition to having his work published in peer-reviewed journals. Jonathan has since left behind his life in academia, moving to Iceland where he now pursues creative endeavors.

His interest in art began with photography which was originally meant as a hobby. This hobby grew into a passion, leading Jonathan to spend considerable time in Europe. During this period, he discovered a love for writing, starting with poetry, then prose — an influence that can be seen in all his written work.

As an artist, Jonathan's motivation is to capture other worlds. As an author, he seeks to create a human world. Utilizing his life experience for perspective, his goal is to inspire others to find meaning and purpose in caring about both themselves and others. Above all else, he seeks to inspire understanding through self-reflection. By encouraging people to explore their inner world, Jonathan hopes to create a more human world.

Additional work and information can be found at:
www.jonathanswerdlow.com

Made in the USA
Columbia, SC
24 July 2024

39300108R00096